THE POLITICS OF

PLEASURE

T0382657

made possible by a generous grant from
THE WILLIAM AND FLORA HEWLETT FOUNDATION

Editors-in-Chief Deborah Chasman & Joshua Cohen

Managing Editor and Arts Editor Adam McGee

Senior Editor Matt Lord

Digital Director Rosie Gillies

Audience Engagement Editor Ben Schacht

Manuscript and Production Editor Hannah Liberman

Contributing Editors Adom Getachew, Lily Hu, Walter Johnson,
Robin D. G. Kelley, Paul Pierson, & Becca Rothfeld

Contributing Arts Editor Ed Pavlić & Ivelisse Rodriguez

Black Voices in the Public Sphere Fellows Maya Jenkins & N'Kosi Oates

Editorial Assistants Milan Kende Loewer & Matene Toure

Special Projects Manager María Clara Cobo

Fellowship Coordinator Jasmine Parmley

Finance Manager Anthony DeMusis III

Printer Sheridan PA

Board of Advisors Derek Schrier (Chair), Archon Fung, Deborah
Fung, Richard M. Locke, Jeff Mayersohn, Jennifer Moses, Scott
Nielsen, Robert Pollin, Rob Reich, Hiram Samel, Kim Malone Scott,
Brandon M. Terry

Interior Graphic Design Zak Jensen & Alex Camlin

Cover Design Alex Camlin

Printed and bound in the United States.

The Politics of Pleasure is *Boston Review* Forum 23 (47.3)

To become a member, visit
bostonreview.net/membership/

For questions about donations and major gifts,
contact Rosie Gillies, rosie@bostonreview.net

For questions about memberships, call 877-406-2443
or email Customer_Service@bostonreview.info

Boston Review
PO Box 390568
Cambridge, MA 02139

ISSN: 0734-2306 / ISBN: 978-1-946511-78-2

CONTENTS

ESSAYS

EDITORS' NOTE
Deborah Chasman & Joshua Cohen

COVID-19 REMAINS a global public health emergency, the planet is on fire, and democracy is at serious risk. Faced with these immense political challenges, why talk about pleasure?

Philosopher Kate Soper has been grappling with this question for decades. As an environmentalist and denuclearization activist, she noticed a worrisome pattern: efforts to green the economy and distribute wealth more equitably often sound like a program for joyless living. Tighten your belt, make do with less, give up your pleasures.

To Soper, this gets it exactly wrong. Leading this issue's forum, she urges that we see "post-growth living" as an opportunity for *greater* pleasure, not less. Modern life is immiserating, sickening, isolating, and exhausting, creating desires that consumption can never fulfill. Designing simpler ways of living—built around local community and abundant free time—could make us happier and healthier while giving our overextended planet a new lease on life.

Forum respondents, including Green New Deal economist Robert Pollin and Kenyan activist Nanjala Nyabola, embrace Soper's call to remake society but question her prescription. The result is a wide-ranging debate about the limitations of lifestyle critique, the value of economic growth, and the kinds of alternatives that are possible.

Among those convinced that pleasure is political was British designer William Morris, a committed socialist and leading figure in the nineteenth-century Arts and Crafts movement. Morris was—as E. P. Thompson once put it—"our greatest diagnostician of alienation." In his essay for this volume, Ben Schacht explores Morris's distinctive vision of a society that prioritizes pleasure and beauty for all.

Other contributions focus on the connections between pleasure and gender, including the joys of collective action and care work, the ordinary pleasures of Black motherhood, and the links between good sex and democracy. Together they imagine what it will take to make a pleasurable life possible for everyone.

FORUM

ALTERNATIVE HEDONISM

Kate Soper

UNTIL RECENTLY, scientific warnings that human activity is causing global warming went largely unheeded. Even less attention was paid to arguments that affluent societies will need to adopt dramatic changes—in consumption, in lifestyle—if they are to bequeath any kind of habitable planet to future generations. On the contrary, environmentalists, green politicians, and their followers were widely ridiculed for being nostalgic, even retrograde. Over the last decade, however, climate science has provided so much evidence of humanly caused global warming—and the resulting floods, fires, and heat waves have become so much more deadly—that the ridicule is now instead aimed at those who had presumed that business would carry on as usual. As for the remaining diehard climate denialists, it is they who are now deemed outside the pale of reason.

Nonetheless, it remains a minority who will readily admit to the role of capitalism and its consumer culture in creating environmental breakdown. It is an even smaller number who dare to suggest that the lifestyle generated through the growth economy is not necessarily the most enjoyable. Climate scientists and many economists now accept the importance of moving away from fossil fuel dependence over time. Some even agree that affluent societies cannot continue in their current ways. But they do so with regret—with a sense that more austere consumption, though necessary, will be to our disadvantage. Even those who are skeptical about the whole project of "green growth," and who quarrel with the cost–benefit calculations used in support of it, too often go along with the consumerist definition of the "benefits" in question. They don't question whether consumption actually benefits us, nor whether, if we consumed differently, the beneficiaries might not only be future generations but we ourselves. Most politicians and business leaders seem likewise incapable of thinking of the "good life" other than in terms of consumerist gratification. Obsessed as they are with economic growth and GDP, they do not invite electorates to entertain other ideas of progress and prosperity, and are more than happy for advertisers to retain their monopoly over how pleasure is imagined. Mainstream politics thus remains dominated by narrow disputes over the means to a commonly agreed set of ends (economic growth, technological development, increased standards of living as defined by current consumer culture).

Nor is this much challenged even by those further to the left, where the tendency to disconnect from issues of material culture has discouraged most from trying to imagine a radically different vision of ethical consumption. Thinkers on the left will agree that capitalist production is a historically specific mode of production, and condemn its human and environmental exploitation. Yet the consumer culture it has bequeathed is often accepted as if it were a natural legacy to be preserved as far as possible—with socialist economics directed at providing its affluence for everyone in abundance. Critics of the current economic order have usually been more bothered about the inequalities of access and distribution it creates than about the ways it confines us to market-driven ways of living. Labor militancy and trade union activity in the West has likewise been largely confined to protection of income and employees' rights within the existing structures of globalized capital, and done little to challenge, let alone transform, the "work and spend" dynamic of affluent cultures. Even among the less pragmatic thinkers on the left—the so-called "tech utopians" and "luxury communists"—something of the consumerist mindset persists. The future that is promised will be more idle (thanks to robots and drones doing most things for us), but it remains conventional in tying much of its pleasure to the continuation of automobile culture and the expanded availability and use of machines and hi-tech gadgetry.

The presumption, however, that more sustainable consumption will always involve sacrifice rather than improve well-being needs challenging. Our so-called "good life" is, after all, a major cause of stress and ill health. It is noisy, polluting, and wasteful. Its work routines and commercial priorities have forced people to plan their whole lives around job-seeking and career. Many are condemned to unfulfilling and precarious work lives in the gig economy. Even those with more secure employment will frequently begin their days in traffic jams or suffering other forms of commuter discomfort, and then spend much of the rest of them glued to a screen engaged in mind-numbing tasks. A good part of their productive activity is designed to lock time into the creation of a material culture of fast fashion, continuous home improvement, urban sprawl, speedier production, and built-in obsolescence.

Our consumption economy's markets profit hugely from selling back to us the goods and services we have too little time or space to provide for ourselves. Consider the role of the fast food, leisure, and therapy industries, or the gyms where people pay to walk on a treadmill because walking anywhere else is impossible or unpleasant. These markets' merchandising strategies promote competitive forms of consumption, especially among the young, often relying on devious means such as body-shaming, thus worsening anxiety and depression. These markets also now subject all online shoppers to the insidious advertising strategies of what has been called "surveillance capitalism," while at the same time off-loading onto the consumer much of the servicing and bureaucracy that businesses used to perform themselves.

Greens, then, may get dismissed as regressive killjoys, and have played into this characterization by presenting reduced consumption as only *necessary* rather than personally rewarding, even pleasurable. But the reality is that today's work-dominated, time-scarce, junk-ridden "affluence" is itself the killjoy, and often puritanical and sensually offensive. Moreover, it does not arise from any innate desire of people constantly to work and consume more. If it did, the billions spent on advertising, and especially on grooming children for a life of consumption, would hardly be necessary.

It may be objected, especially in these times of intense economic hardship for so many, that in advocating the pleasures of escaping the consumerist lifestyle, I overlook how partial the access to its forms of affluence has actually been. What sense, it will be asked, can my argument have for those increasing numbers who currently wonder how they will provide even such basics as food, clothing, and heat. Critics may rightly note that even in better times, few have ever really been in a position to enjoy much of the comfort or luxury associated with affluence. I am sensitive to these objections. But they overlook the extent to which the consumerist lifestyle functions in affluent societies as a regime in which we are all caught up, whatever our income. Viewed in this light, people who are on the breadline, or only just managing, have not escaped the constraints of its work ethic or on what they can do and how. All are subject to them. Even among the adequately employed, most have too little time and not enough income to consume more sustainably even if they want to. Hence their reliance on buying ready meals or processed food, quick air flights for compressed family vacations, cheap goods from Amazon, and so forth.

Consumer society is, in this sense, itself a vehicle of inequality and the provider of a distinctive form and aesthetic of material culture to which we must all, in one way or another, conform. Although often acclaimed as the guarantor of universal freedom and self-expression, it might be better viewed at this stage in its evolution as a means of extending the global reach and command of corporate power at the expense of the health and well-being of both the planet and the majority of Earth's inhabitants. In exchange for this misery, it offers the "compensation" of goods and services which, though intensely profitable for corporations, fall far short of making up for what has been lost through overwork. Considered in this light, we should not think of the changes forced by the climate crisis as a disaster, but rather as an opportunity to embrace a fairer, more enticing way of living.

I would respond along similar lines to the equally relevant objection that my argument overlooks the importance of a continuing growth economy in meeting the needs of those in so-called underdeveloped or developing nations. I accept that economic growth will be needed in the short term to ensure the provision of basic needs in the poorest nations. I also agree with economist Kate Raworth that growth may temporarily result from measures undertaken to secure a "regenerative and distributive" economy—for example, to establish an infrastructure for renewable energy. But the overall aim must be to wrest control of global wealth and material resources from the grip—and accompanying ecological dereliction—of a relatively small corporate elite. Between 1990 and 2015, the world's richest 10 percent produced over half of all carbon emissions while the poorest 50 percent produced less than a tenth. It is also the poorer nations who are doing the least to create climate breakdown yet who are suffering most severely from its social and environmental impacts.

It is therefore absurd that nations whose citizens' consumption grossly exceeds the planet's carrying capacity should continue to be held out as aspirational models for the rest of the world. Capitalist-driven consumer culture should no longer be allowed to exercise its monopoly over conceptions of well-being and how to secure it. Indeed, societies with traditions of less industrialized but more sustainable methods of production and modes of consuming must surely begin to count as more progressive. This has long been recognized by many indigenous activists and critics of the current neoliberal thinking on development. In the words, for example, of Nemonte Nenquimo, cofounder of the indigenous nonprofit organization Ceibo Alliance, and first female president of the Waorani organization in the Ecuadorian Amazon:

> You forced your civilisation upon us, and now look where we are: global pandemic, climate crisis, species extinction and, driving it all, widespread spiritual poverty. In all these years of taking, taking, taking from our lands, you have not had the courage, or the curiosity, or the respect to get to know us. To understand how we see, and think, and feel, and what we know about life on this Earth.

In line with this, in my book *Post-Growth Living* (2020) I emphasize the need to revise and revalue concepts of prosperity and development in order to bring them more in line with the more sustainable ways of living and working that have so often been swept aside by capitalist "progress." This would not endorse a "back to nature" ethic through which modern "excesses" could be corrected by return to a "simple" way of life. But it would resist the presentism that refuses to look to the past for resources that could help us form a more viable, enjoyable future.

Concerned consumers in more affluent societies must lead the way in this rethinking and thus act as an essential initial leverage for a global green renaissance. The Debt for Climate campaign rightly proposes a global revolt against debt and austerity in which poor world governments refuse to honor their debts and activists in the rich world support them by calling for debt cancellation as well as reparations for the devastating loss and damage caused by our greenhouse gas emissions. As George Monbiot has put it in a recent article: "By reviving the question of who owes what to whom, huge constituencies, labour and green, north and south, can develop a common platform. Climate campaigns are indivisible from global justice."

WE NEED to be more assertively utopian in promoting sustainable consumption in richer nations. I don't mean only that our blueprints must be more openly utopian in the futures they plan for, but that we must also actively encourage desires and feelings to match. The new consumption is not a matter of simplifying needs and wants. Rather, we want a world that provides *more* of what we currently lack, and which opens the way to previously unconceived experiences. In what follows I explore this idea by charting (in a necessarily incomplete way) some of the losses and gains that might follow were we to embrace a new vision of consumption which I call "alternative hedonism."

Work

WERE WE TO SPEND less time working—committing, say, to a three- or four-day workweek—the workaholics might lose some of the gratifications of a 24/7 job-centered lifestyle. But many people would be spared the hassle and expense of daily commuting and the long hours spent on it. They would avoid much of the stress and stress-related illnesses incurred through overwork. The large numbers now employed in financial and administrative services, described by anthropologist David Graeber as often spending "their entire working lives performing tasks they secretly believe do not really need to be performed," would be saved from the futility of their "bullshit jobs." The less skilled or formally qualified workers of the precariat, who are both exposed to the instability of the gig economy and deprived of occupational identity or career trajectory, would likewise escape from the insecurity and demeaning forms of discipline associated with dead-end work.

In a working culture no longer dominated by profit-driven ideas of efficiency, we could reintroduce traditional artisanal modes of production which fell out of favor because they are slower, while employing the smartest, greenest technologies in those industries where such methods of production would not be suitable (energy and medicine, for example). Methods of production that featured closed-loop cycles of resource use, and which gave priority to upcycling over recycling, would put an end to built-in obsolescence and radically reduce waste.

Artisanal "slow working" could make space in some areas of production for those currently excluded by age or disability, and help to enhance job fulfilment. Let us add to this the greater pleasure that people would experience knowing that their work no longer contributed to environmental breakdown, nor threatened the very survival of their children and grandchildren. Such a shift would also put an end to many of the more dispiriting jobs—those, for example, devoted purely to brand enhancement and the merchandising activities that go with it.

The reduction in work would necessarily need to proceed in tandem with the introduction of some form of citizens' or universal basic income. This would allow people to make good use of their increase in free time, and make them better able to enjoy the novel forms of cooperative consumption and conviviality it could promote. It would also lessen inequalities and help to promote a less gendered, racialized, and class-based division of labor. Society would necessarily shift from a work-centered understanding of identity, purpose, and self-fulfillment to one that revolved around more self-chosen ways of spending time and energy. In turn, the work ethic that so stigmatizes the unemployed would loosen its grip, and more encouragement could be given to self-provisioning, as well as to craft-based and cultural activities, games, hobbies, and other intrinsically valued ways of spending time.

Educational priorities would need to be revised accordingly, with a shift from a too purely vocational focus—education as preparation for work and career—to one that made space for instruction that enhanced the enjoyment of free time. This would extend from elementary school through to higher education and beyond. As much time would be given in schools to music, dance, drama, painting, and literature as to the scientific and technical subjects. The humanities would in the process be restored from their rather marginal status, as appreciation grew for how they support non-instrumental values and provide critical resources unavailable through other subject areas.

Soper

When well taught, the humanities challenge comfortable convictions, thus advancing a more historical, intersubjective, critically honed sense of one's own identity and place in society.

Travel

WERE WE TO CURB dependency on cars and airplanes, we would lose the thrills and convenience of very fast transport. To many Americans, this will seem likely to reduce their pleasure and comfort as well as being financially impossible. Nor, perhaps, will many pay much attention to the now all too familiar advice that we should restrict our use of planes and automobiles so as to offset the destabilizing global impacts of fossil fuel reliance.

In response, however, to the objection that other modes of travel are too expensive to be realistic alternatives, it is worth noting that they would become less expensive were we to use them more: were demand for trains and boats to increase, for example, the costs of such journeys would decrease. Already in Europe, many longer journeys by train cost little more than scheduled flights, save around 90 percent of carbon emissions, and can in some cases take scarcely any more time than flying when journey to airports and preflight waiting times are added on.

But there are advantages beyond the financial, as well. Train and boat travel can provide a richer and more engaged experience of the regions through which one is traveling. Far-flung vacations have become very popular, but they do not always live up to their promise of providing exceptional experiences and can leave travelers exhausted. Vacations taken closer to home—and without the high stakes of needing to generate memories to last a lifetime—may provide unexpected forms of enchantment and serve just as well as escapes from mundanity.

In addition to its carbon emissions, automobile transport has a massive impact on air pollution. Some 300 million children now live in areas where toxic fumes are 6 times above international guidelines, and almost all the global adult population is now affected to some degree. Hybrid and fully electric vehicles will reduce pollution, but large amounts of plastic are still involved in their construction, the electricity they use must be generated, and their batteries need to be sustainably produced and safely discarded. Nor will they necessarily do much to spare us the accidents that are responsible for so much death and maiming (nearly 39,000 lost their lives in traffic accidents in the United States in 2020). Electric machines will also do nothing to lessen congestion or the automobile's colonization of urban space. Instead, electric vehicles look set to protract the dangers and spatial monopoly of car culture, rather than moving us beyond its mindset.

Road transport is also a significant cause of wildlife and ecosystem destruction at a time when we have been warned that everything now needs to be done to improve conservation. Screened as its users are from the external impact of speed, they are insensitive to its environmental devastation, and cut off from many of the aesthetic pleasures of slower and less insulated modes of traveling. They are confined to what Alexander Wilson, in his 1991 study *The Culture of Nature* about the making of the North American landscape, called the "motorist's aesthetic": a purely visual experience comparable in its two-dimensionality to the view that is had in aerial photography. Scenic routes, Wilson suggests, have instructed generations of drivers in a flattened idea of nature's "beauty" by "removing whatever bits of it were deemed unsightly, and by restricting all activities incompatible with the parkway aesthetic." It is a too purely visual aesthetic that has been further reinforced through modern media, since so many now experience "nature" primarily as something seen on TV or screens.

Automobile culture also deprives us of the positive enjoyments of ambling and gossiping and passing the day in urban space. As the Living Streets campaigners have pointed out, urban space used to be mainly devoted to socializing, public meetings, entertainment, demonstrations, and social change. Today much of it is given over to car traffic, cutting swathes through communities. Children have been deprived of safe urban places in which to play, adults are discouraged from idling in the street. Doing so has acquired the negative connotation of "loitering," which many jurisdictions have even criminalized. Many of what pass for "public" spaces are, in fact, often privately owned and policed—shopping malls and outlets, for instance—and though they at least offer protection from traffic, the more "disreputable" (non-shopping) elements are under continual surveillance and regularly moved on. Nor is seating much in evidence lest non-shoppers take advantage.

Were we to reverse these trends—as some cities are now belatedly beginning to do—then we could readily provide for safe transit for pedestrians and cyclists. This would enable far more people to enjoy sights, scents, sounds, and pleasures—not to mention health benefits—

of physical activity. Walking and biking can offer a balm of solitude and silence denied to those who travel in noisier, speedier ways. Freed from traffic dangers, children could come out to play again, and walk or cycle to school. Such provision could take quite baroque forms: multi-lane tracks with handsome colonnades and covered routes for protection from the weather, cycle rickshaws and electric bikes for the too young and less able, showers and changing rooms and cafes at regular intervals on cycle tracks. Utopian as they may currently seem, the costs of such schemes would be small relative to that of continued expansion of autoroutes—especially if one factors in the medical costs likely to be saved through better public health and fewer accidents.

Shopping

IF WE WERE TO SHIFT to a less acquisitive consumer culture—shopping less and committing to more self-provisioning, mending, and making do—we would miss out on the use of consumption for self-display and status signaling. There would be less stuff in our lives; we would have to forego the enticements of following fashion; we would lose the convenience of Walmart and Amazon.

Conspicuous or invidious consumption (the buying of goods to gain the attention or envy of others) has certainly proved compelling, and expanded the market in many goods, especially in clothing, household furnishings, and electronic equipment. It has thus served the growth economy extremely well. But its gratifications for consumers are complicated by what has come to be known as "hedonic adaptation" and the "hedonic treadmill." Research suggests that the pleasures of acquisition are not enhanced beyond a certain point, whatever the material gains, while the competitive desire for status goods is like a treadmill: since all are continuously vying to keep up with each other's acquisitions, no one is finally satisfied.

Similarly, fashion seems to offer ever-changing opportunities to express individuality, but what it actually generates are waves of conformity to whatever is promoted on the market. A promise of self-realization is held out, but only on the condition that you submit to the dictate of a collectivity you have neither willed nor authored. The fashion industry strives to make essentially homogeneous forms of consumption seem constantly innovative and therefore desirable, but does little to promote genuine difference and eccentricity. The result, moreover, is environmentally disastrous. The average American consumer nearly doubled the amount of apparel bought annually between 1991 and 2006. Worldwide over 100 billion items of clothing are produced annually, with brands shoveling excess production into incinerators. A similar logic of fashionable design has developed in IT markets, whose discarded items are now contributing to the fastest growing forms of waste, much of it highly toxic, across the Western world.

To reduce dependence on these sources of gratification would, then, greatly cut down on waste. It would spare us the intrusive and often unsightly sprawl of the hypermarkets and fulfilment centers, and lessen the clutter in homes. In compensation, communal ways of meeting needs might emerge and offer alternative forms of enjoyment. Local cooperatives and social enterprises could expand.

So, too, could all those modes of acquisition and consumption that bypass the market or allow people to satisfy their requirements for goods and services without purchasing new commodities from commercial suppliers. These include sharing schemes, flea markets, charity and secondhand shops, and all the resources for the recycling of articles—for which there are now a growing number of websites. Apart from the pleasures of person-to-person reciprocity, such exchanges and bartering activities save money and allow people to make use of specific talents and eccentric interests for which they may otherwise have little outlet. The provision of hubs for the hiring, borrowing, and sharing of vehicles, tools, and educational and financial services—not to mention arts centers, supper clubs, and the like—would transform main streets and city centers, and encourage new forms of citizenship (and the pleasures that go with that). It could also lessen isolation for the elderly and lonely by opening up spaces and opportunities for more street conviviality. Allotments and gardens would likely multiply, with more people enjoying the pleasures of growing and eating their own food.

SKEPTICS WILL DOUBT that these more sustainable forms of pleasure can substitute for those of consumerist lifestyles, or win sufficient support to exercise political leverage over the current economic order. It is true that the absence to date of any serious consumer revolt in affluent societies indicates that most at least tolerate, if not actively support, the consumerist way of living. Moreover, although corporate power is extensive and exercises a massive influence on the production and marketing of goods and services, it would be a mistake to present the environmental troubles of our times as entirely accountable to the providing industries and their merchandising manipulations. The appetites of customers in rich nations, and the priority given to their convenience, play a major role, too, and any advocacy of degrowth and a more peaceful, sharing economic order will need to recognize that—particularly if we are to reduce our fossil fuel dependency. To treat "us," the general public in affluent societies, as victims of "their" entrepreneurial activities is to offer too comforting an escape. The numbers who express concern over the environmental horrors per-petrated by corporate power and government hardly seem matched at present by changes in individual consumer behavior—or indeed in voting patterns.

As the COVID-19 pandemic has run its course, however, signs have emerged that this hitherto broadly shared agreement on the lifestyle we want to preserve may be beginning to fracture. The postconsumerist arguments of previously disregarded groups (such as the Degrowth network and the Next System Project) are finding more traction in the mainstream. So, too, are those of green parties and NGOs campaigning not only for a recommitment to ideas of the commons, and a more participatory economic order, but also for the necessary preceding step of revising how we connect well-being with consumption.

The war in Ukraine has also opened more eyes to the dangers of a world order dominated by the producers of fossil fuels, too accommodating of the nationalism of kleptocrats, and relatively indifferent toward environmental breakdown. Such pressures might mean that the downsides of our fast-paced, acquisitive lifestyle, voiced only by a minority at present, come over time to receive more mainstream support.

That people hanker after something else, and would enjoy it more, has also long had the backing of research studies showing that more wealth does not necessarily make you happier, and that the pursuit of ever more consumption is inherently self-defeating. It is true that such research needs to be treated with caution. Among the complicating factors, the degree of satisfaction people self-report often has little to do with how they are actually faring. Nor does a lack of correlation between higher income and self-reported satisfaction mean that more consumption has not improved a person's well-being. There are likely many reasons for this disjunct. The standards people use to assess their satisfaction may become more stringent as their wealth increases. Education made available by wealth can improve an individual's sense of freedom and personal potential precisely by generating discontent with her existing life situation.

These issues raise questions as to what should count in the estimation of the "good life." Is it the intensity of its more isolated moments of pleasure, or overall level of contentment? Is it the avoidance of pain and difficulty, or successfully overcoming those? And who is best placed to decide on whether personal well-being has increased? Is this entirely a matter of subjective self-reporting, or open to more objective appraisal? Those defending a more objective assessment will point out, first, that people are not always the best judges of their own well-being and, second, that much immediate pleasure can be had from behaviors that are self-destructive or environmentally vandalizing. Relatedly, it has been claimed that a "happiness" conceived or measured in terms of subjective feeling discourages the development of the sense of citizenship and intergenerational solidarity essential to social and environmental well-being.

There is, then, a tension in discussions of hedonism and the good life between privileging a subjective sense of pleasure and reaching for a more objective understanding. Where the former risks overlooking the critical long-term links between the "good life" and the "good society," the latter runs the risk of being patronizing by suggesting that "experts" understand our own happiness better than we do. Yet the more subjective approach need not exclude the civically oriented forms of pleasure that come with consuming in ways that are responsible to others and to the environment. After all, the pleasure of many activities—riding a bike, for example—consists both in the more immediately personal sensual enjoyments *and* in the pleasure of not contributing to the vices of car culture, including pollution and urban fragmentation.

In the end, no legitimate claim about someone's well-being or degree of life satisfaction is possible without some endorsement from the individual in question. It is, however, one thing to accept the complexity of gauging claims about quality of life and personal satisfaction. It is another to deny the evidence of the self-defeating nature of ever-expanding consumption. My alternative hedonism cannot—and does not aspire to—resolve the philosophical issues in this area. Instead, I seek to make clearer the yearnings for alternative ways of living that are implied by emergent disaffection with affluent culture, and point to what they instruct us about pleasure and well-being. My main interest is thus, to invoke a concept of cultural critic Raymond Williams, in a "structure of feeling"—that is, a popular, though still nascent, intuition in the back of people's minds that something about our conventional life has gone wrong and must change. For me, this "structure of feeling" points toward a postconsumerist vision of the "good life." My alternative hedonism aims to avoid moralizing about what people ought to need or want—even if a certain amount of that is unavoidable—while still troubling the forms of consumption that have been taken for granted. I hope, so doing, to draw attention to former pleasures gone missing, and to issue a compelling summons to another way of living.

As the planet heats, we need a political response appealing to, and supported by, this "structure of feeling." It must challenge the stranglehold of the work ethic on the Western way of life, and seek to replace it with a socioeconomic order in which work and income are more fairly distributed, coparenting and part-time work become the norm, and everyone has the means and time for sustainable forms of activity and life-enhancement. Doing so could transform urban and rural living, especially for children, and provide more tranquil space for reflection, offering opportunities for sensual experience denied by harried travel and work routines. It would also help to lay the groundwork for a more egalitarian and peaceful world order.

There are some conveniences and pleasures of affluent living that would have to be sacrificed in a low-carbon economy: creature comforts of various kinds; some of the thrills of fast-paced living; the ease with which we have recently gratified the passion for foreign travel. Shifting to a postconsumerist way of living is also a daunting prospect in view of the integrated structure of modern existence and the subordination of national economies to the globalized system. Yet it is also unrealistic to suppose that we can continue with the current rates of expansion of production, work, and consumption over coming decades, let alone into the next century and beyond. Greener technologies will help to counter global warming. But the implementation of alternatives to the growth economy must become central to planning and policy-making, rather than ignored or dismissed as unworkable fantasy.

My argument for alternative hedonism is frequently rejected as unrealistic. I counter that it is, instead, quite seriously implausible that the future can be "business as usual." There is an urgent need for a politics of prosperity that dissociates pleasure and fulfilment from resource-intensive consumption. And in doing so, it is important to avoid fanciful assumptions about what would constitute globally sustainable forms of industry and lifestyle. Such a vision must be what frames our discussions of how work, politics, and economics will look in a socially just and viable future.

THE DEGROWTH ECONOMY
Robert Pollin

KATE SOPER PRESENTS an excellent overview of her "assertively utopian" vision of a "postconsumerist way of living" in which people spend less time working, traveling great distances in cars and airplanes, and shopping on the "hedonic treadmill" for things they don't need.

I fully support Soper's utopian vision. But that is easy to do. Her vision will be unobjectionable to most people holding even vaguely progressive sympathies. Matters only get complicated when we ask how we can most effectively transition to the good society that Soper describes, given the hard realities of where things stand in the world today.

Let's start with terminology. An increasing number of commentators have embraced the term "degrowth" to describe the trajectory for achieving something akin to Soper's good society. Soper herself seems to prefer the term "post-growth." I think we should worry less about labels and instead focus on what should constitute the substance of this egalitarian and ecologically sustainable society. Scrutinized in this way, the fundamental issue ceases to be economic growth per se, in any and all forms. Rather, we should expect that some economic activities within the good society should grow—for example, environmental protection, primary education, and elder care—while others should remain stable, and still others should either contract or be eliminated altogether. The real challenge becomes figuring out which activities go into each of these categories.

When it comes to the climate crisis, in particular, I think we can accomplish much more through trying to focus on which activities need to grow versus those that need to contract. Here are a few key specifics. The Intergovernmental Panel on Climate Change (IPCC) estimates that for the global economy to move onto a viable climate stabilization path, global emissions of carbon dioxide (CO_2) will have to fall by about 45 percent as of 2030—only a little more than seven years from now—and reach net zero emissions by 2050. As such, the core of a unified climate stabilization and egalitarian project—what we can term a global Green New Deal—has to be, first, to hit the IPCC CO_2 emissions reduction targets, and then, second, to accomplish this in a way that also expands decent job opportunities and raises mass living standards throughout the world.

Within this overarching project, the single most important action must be to phase out the consumption of oil, coal, and natural gas for energy production, which accounts for about 70–75 percent of all global CO_2 emissions. In short, fossil fuel energy consumption needs to "de-grow" to zero. Of course, achieving such a transformation will mean a massive, uphill political war, given the huge global power of both the public and private oil companies. But there is no alternative to winning this struggle if we have any chance of saving the planet.

As the fossil fuel energy infrastructure phases down to zero by 2050, we concurrently have to build an entirely new global energy infrastructure whose centerpieces will be high efficiency and clean renewable energy sources—primarily solar and wind power. People are obviously still going to need to consume energy, from any available source, to light, heat, and cool buildings; to power cars, buses, trains, and airplanes; and to operate computers and industrial machinery, among other uses. Moreover, any minimally decent global egalitarian program will entail a significant increase in energy consumption for lower-income people throughout the world.

How much would cutting back on overall economic growth—moving onto a degrowth or post-growth trajectory—contribute toward delivering a zero-emissions global economy? The answer is: very little. COVID-19 lockdowns around the world provided a powerful natural experiment to demonstrate this point. In 2020 the global economy contracted by 3.5 percent, which the International Monetary Fund described as a "severe collapse . . . that has had acute adverse impacts on women, youth, the poor, the informally employed and those who work in contact-intensive sectors." In other words, the pandemic produced an intense period of global degrowth. This recession also produced a decline in emissions, as entire sections of the global economy were forced into lockdown mode. But the emissions decline amounted to only 6.4 percent over 2020. If the pandemic recession only yields a 6.4 percent emissions reduction despite the enormous levels of economic pain inflicted, clearly degrowth cannot come close, on its own, to delivering a 45 percent emissions cut by 2030, much less a zero emissions global economy by 2050.

By contrast, a strategy focused on growing the right parts of the economy will pay dividends. Investing in the improvement of energy efficiency standards and the expansion of the global supply of clean energy sources will not only reduce emissions; it will also create millions of jobs, in all regions of the world. Of course, there is no guarantee that these new jobs will be good jobs: after all, we are still operating within capitalism. Climate activists therefore need to join forces with unions and other labor organizers to fight for good wages, benefits, and safe and equitable working conditions. At the same time, the phasing out of the global fossil fuel industry will mean large-scale losses for workers and communities that are presently dependent on the fossil fuel industry. Providing a just transition for these workers and communities also needs to be at the center of the egalitarian climate stabilization project.

For over a decade, labor activists, such as those associated with the Labor Network for Sustainability in the United States, have been organizing around these issues. Against steep odds, they have started to win some significant victories, including an endorsement for a robust green investment and just transition program in California by the union representing the state's oil refinery workers. Rather than recognizing these challenges and achievements, Soper criticizes union movements in the West for being "confined to protection of income and employees' rights within the existing structure of globalized capital" and for doing "little to challenge, let alone transform, the 'work and spend' dynamic of affluent cultures." It is fair to ask what Soper would say to the California oil refinery workers. Would she have the union leaders deemphasize the demand for guaranteed new jobs at equal pay for all displaced fossil fuel workers? Would she instead give priority to explaining how much better the workers' lives might be in a future post-growth society?

Soper says she is sensitive to the objection that "in advocating the pleasures of escaping the consumerist lifestyle, I overlook how partial the access to its forms of affluence has actually been." Soper similarly recognizes that "economic growth will be needed in the short term to ensure the provision of basic needs in the poorest nations." But she offers no specifics as to how short her "short term" should be, what countries or communities should get included in her category of "the poorest nations," and what should constitute the "basic needs" of these countries or communities. These are critical questions that require clarity.

To take one pertinent example: average daily temperatures were sustained at over 110° Fahrenheit during the heat wave in India this past May. The intensifying climate crisis is making such episodes increasingly frequent. One obvious way to protect people during heat waves is with air conditioning. However, only 8 percent of Indian households now own air conditioning units. The situation in most of the rest of the world is not that different from India. The climate crisis has made access to air conditioning—along with cheap electricity to power the units—a necessity.

Delivering this basic form of protection on a global basis will obviously require major investments on a global scale. Energy consumption will rise and, along with it, consumption of all kinds of related goods and services. I cannot see any ethical path to achieving the society Soper describes unless we demonstrate an unequivocal commitment to improving people's lives right now in today's world.

THE FULLNESS OF DESIRE
Lida Maxwell

THE DOMINANT CONCEPTION of happiness in the United States is unabashedly acquisitive. It involves marriage (or at least being coupled), probably children, probably homeownership, and definitely easy and ongoing consumption. This idea of bourgeois happiness is powerfully connected, as Kate Soper argues, to capitalism. Yet it is also connected to patriarchy and to white supremacy. As Lori Marso has argued, the sparkly consumer objects and material splendor promised by the "bourgeois respectability" of marriage offer compensation for women's lack of freedom. And, of course, the idea of bourgeois happiness, as thinkers from W. E. B. Du Bois to Audre Lorde have argued, is deeply entwined with white supremacy. This is why, as James Baldwin wrote in *Giovanni's Room* (1956) and *The Fire Next Time* (1963), this idea or fantasy of white happiness is actually a kind of depravity: it allows, even requires, white people to look away from the reality of white supremacy, racial violence, and sexual domination that produces their lives.

Soper's call to develop and nurture an alternative hedonism is an important intervention. She is right that Westerners tend to have a very narrow idea of happiness, even as our attachment to this idea often makes us unhappy and continues to drive climate change. As long as the habits and structures of consumption endure, climate change will become more and more catastrophic.

I am less convinced than Soper, though, that focusing on changing habits and infrastructures of *consumption* offers a robust enough idea of either pleasure or political action to address climate change. Part of capitalism's magic, after all, is inculcating a particular experience of desire in us—teaching us that we have an inherent void or lack that must be filled for us to be happy, to experience pleasure. As Lauren Berlant argued, we learn to experience our endless disappointments as due to our own failures, to the disappointments of love or intimacy or the family—and not to the structural unhappiness of capitalism. The suffering and unhappiness of Black, brown, and poor people is portrayed in this ideology as their own doing, due to their own personal failures—or, at best, as something that well-off white people can or should *sympathize* with, feel virtuously on behalf of.

While capitalism tells us that we should try to fill our void with bourgeois marriage, work, virtuous sympathy, and endless consumption, Soper tells us we should try to fill our void with crafts, localism, and sharing economies. I agree that we might arrange our lives differently, but her call to simply change our habits of consumption does not go far enough. If we don't challenge the very idea of desire as a void to be filled, we risk advocating a politics that remains principally white, non-feminist, and heteronormative.

Maxwell

Only a different vision of desire—desire as fullness—can ground a politics up to the task of dismantling the drivers of climate change, patriarchy, and white supremacy.

There are many model for the conception of desire as fullness, for example, in the writings of Baldwin (especially "My Dungeon Shook") and Lorde (especially "Uses of the Erotic: The Erotic as Power") as well as in Melissa Broder's *Milkfed* (2021), the writings and podcasts of activist adrienne maree brown, and in the poetry of Natalie Diaz and Donika Kelly (among others). In my own work on Rachel Carson and the politics of queer love and climate change, I foreground a conception of desire born out of experiences of intimate pleasure and fullness. My work focuses on Carson's love with Dorothy Freeman that developed in the mid- to late 1950s, and its role in her writing of *Silent Spring* (1962). Carson and Freeman's love, and the birds and other nonhuman nature that made that love possible, showed Carson that a vibrant multispecies world was already a place where people could—and do—experience pleasure and happiness. While many see *Silent Spring* as a plea for humans to remove themselves from nature, I see it as a plea to sustain and amplify a vibrant multispecies world where human happiness is possible, but which was under threat by an unregulated chemical industry.

Desire as lack teaches people that they need particular things (endless consumption) or structures (bourgeois marriage) or feelings (heteronormative love), which may never fully arrive, to be happy. In contrast, desire as *fullness* teaches people that they already have the capacity for pleasure in themselves and in this world and thus gives critical distance from capitalist, heteronormative institutions that had once seemed necessary to happiness. In desire as lack, people are taught that they and their private lives are the reason for their unhappiness, which helps shore up the status quo. In desire as fullness, social and political structures appear as the reason that happiness and pleasure are under threat. Desire as fullness thus directs our political attention to collective conditions and political structures, while desire as lack keeps us focused on our internal and private lives.

I see desire as fullness as more politically potent, especially in addressing climate change, because it starts to undo the capitalist indoctrination of lack. Desire as fullness also generates greater political capacity, courage, and confidence because it teaches people that they can achieve their desires, even if they do not accord with capitalist common sense. Carson and Freeman's love served as a spark for Carson's *Silent Spring*, as well as for her broad work in coalition-building to push for greater regulation of the chemical industry. In that book and her other late work, we see her most searing indictments of capitalism and industry and their attempted destruction of pleasurable lives. We also see her greatest political courage in this time of her life, when she fought the smears against her in print and in person and made numerous appearances (including in front of the Senate) to speak on behalf of greater regulation, even as she was dying of breast cancer.

At a time when political institutions seem rigidly entrenched in a growth economy that is killing us, Soper is right that we need to imagine utopic futures of travel, work, and consumption. But we also need to find ways to undo our experiences of ourselves as beings of lack and start to identify and experience moments of desire as fullness that can ground a new politics. Desire as fullness can spark forms of movement-building and political agency that might achieve these utopic goals.

Imagine desire as fullness as that spark for a new climate politics: experiences of pleasure and happiness reveal that we are not lacking beings, and this leads to greater courage and bigger goals for our lives and world during climate change, a greater sense of what is possible.

If engaging in this kind of politics is hard to imagine, it is because we have been so stuck in a politics of intimate lack for so long. We have been led to doubt our capacity to achieve change and to diminish our desires to small demands for better consumption and minimum protections for life. It will take a lot to undo this, but part of it—as Soper rightly notes—is an intimate project. Experiences of fullness create greater clarity about the depravity of capitalism, as well as greater political capacity, courage, and imagination. We need an intimate politics of climate change that begins from the fullness of our capacity for pleasure. Only then will our democratic politics expand beyond demands for individual bare survival to the fullness of pleasurable lives for everyone.

ECOLOGY'S UTOPIAN VISION
Jackson Lears

KATE SOPER'S PLEA for an "alternative hedonism" is cogent, necessary, and brave. It has been absent from public debate for far too long. She revives an argument that began to disappear almost fifty years ago. Mid-century environmental thinkers like E. F. Schumacher had recognized that life under a regime of relentless economic growth was anything but the fun its promoters in the advertising business claimed. For Schumacher and the early ecological movement, the phrase "hedonistic consumer culture" was an oxymoron. High consumption required high production, which in turn depended on labor discipline; the managers of the system created a squirrel cage of earning and spending. From the ecological view, escape from the cage could open possibilities for a more fulfilling way of life—a slowing of the pace that could open up and resurrect possibilities for personal reflection and spontaneous sociability, an alternative hedonism.

The countercultural ecology of the early seventies emphasized the centrality of conservation, which blended pragmatic necessity and utopian promise. If we weaned ourselves away from a wasteful, throwaway culture, we might not only save the planet but also locate more enjoyable ways of living on it. This assumption was taken for granted in the environmental movement, which included more than a few hedonists seeking a sensuously, aesthetically, and spiritually satisfying life.

Yet within a few years after the publication of Schumacher's *Small Is Beautiful* in 1973, the assumption that conservation complemented hedonism had nearly disappeared from U.S. public discourse. A seismic shift had occurred, and ideological positions had been rearranged. Even people who considered themselves leftists began to harbor suspicions of environmentalists' alleged asceticism. The key ideological move was the resurrection of the familiar claim that consumer culture was a riot of hedonistic pleasure-seeking. From this view, it became easy to dismiss environmentalists as killjoys who didn't know a cookin' party when they saw one. And this revaluation of consumption accompanied a broader retreat from conservation. By the end of the century, U.S. highways were filled with thundering herds of sport utility vehicles whose emission standards were looser because they were officially defined as trucks. Hard to know what happened to all those conservationists seeking fuel-efficient cars in the seventies.

The marginalizing of environmental concerns lasted for decades and delayed any serious attention to global warming and other catastrophic developments. How could this have happened? Any explanation would involve stirring through a complex blend of political, cultural, economic, and technological change. In 1979, when Americans had been struggling with a stagnant job market, gas lines, and lower household temperatures for years, President Jimmy Carter addressed the nation on the need for limits. Limited economic growth meant reducing oil and gas usage as well as wearing sweaters inside, for example. These were hardly privations, but from a let-'er-rip consumerist point of view, the speech could be deemed puritanical. Certainly Carter made no mention of an alternative hedonism in his regime of limits.

Yet polls indicated that the public response was initially receptive to Carter's rhetoric of sacrifice. It was only after the Washington press corps began to natter away about the president's allegedly dour demeanor that his support began to sink. Ronald Reagan was waiting in the wings, crowning his victory over Carter with the slogan "America is back!" Reagan's America was about nothing if not transcending limits, especially limits to endless economic growth. Accumulation and display were back.

Reagan accelerated the neoliberal turn that Carter had begun, embracing the supposed needs of "the free market" as the criteria for evaluating policy decisions. Environmental regulators were brought under scrutiny; regulators were forced to justify their existence. "New Democrats" began to wade into the murky waters of neoliberalism. A left-Reaganism emerged, celebrating its own hip version of the neoliberal self, which created an identity through the assemblage of consumer goods.

The neoliberal self spent a lot of time staring into screens, as the rise of the personal computer completed the dissolution of ecology's utopian vision. Corporate visionaries believed that the unleashed power of cybertechnology, underwritten by deregulated capital, was creating what Bill Gates called a "friction-free" economy, where desire could possess its object with the click of a mouse. Computers were essential to this system.

More important, computers could be cool. As Fred Turner showed in *From Counterculture to Cyberculture* (2006), the success of entrepreneurs like Stewart Brand (creator of the *Whole Earth Catalogue*) fueled a resurgent technophilia. This outlook eventually supplanted countercultural skepticism toward technology with a new-style environmentalism that depended on technical solutions, which in turn required acquisition of the latest techno-gear. Through the efforts of Steve Jobs, Tracy Kidder, and other cyber gurus, computers were transformed and rebranded: from impersonal room-size instruments of corporate uniformity to desk-size, lap-size, and eventually pocket-size agents of personal liberation. Kidder's *The Soul of a New Machine* (1980) signaled the onset of the iconic reversal: the emblem of the soulless bureaucracy became ensouled, an engine of enchantment. Such notions have besotted technophiles for decades.

The disappearance of conservation from ecological discourse has restricted environmental solutions to the realm of the merely technical, such as a focus on the importance of shifting from gasoline-powered to electric cars. As Soper suggests, there is a certain self-deception involved in the single-minded focus on moving from fossil fuel to solar-powered electricity: it allows affluent consumers who consider themselves environmentally conscious to preserve their wired, frequent-flyer way of life. Soper persuasively argues that this way of life itself is part of the problem—and that conservation, not merely techno-fixes, must be part of the solution.

Soper admirably emphasizes the international dimensions of the struggle for ecological survival, keeping the need to address grotesque inequalities in clear view. My only concern is with her brief and inadequate mention of the Ukraine war. Its consequences are far more serious and wide-ranging, with respect to climate crisis, than she acknowledges. Recognizing this requires a clearer understanding of the war than the Western media version. While we deplore the Russian invasion, we must acknowledge it was provoked—by decades of U.S.-led NATO expansion to the East, by a U.S.-supported coup in 2014 which placed hard-right nationalists in positions of power, and by eight years of U.S.-backed Ukrainian war on Russian speakers in the Donbass. U.S. foreign policy has been captured by messianic ideologues who want to use Ukraine to fight a proxy war against Putin. The ultimate aim, says Secretary of Defense Lloyd Austin, is a "weakened" Russia. China is next. There is no apparent limit to the reassertion of U.S.–NATO hegemony. An alliance once supposedly focused on the North Atlantic is now being expanded to include the South China Sea. Elite policymakers are maneuvering the world into heavily armed camps.

What does this have to do with ecological crisis? Everything, unfortunately. At the very least, the U.S.–NATO conjuring of demonic Eurasian rivals distracts attention and redirects resources away from crucial efforts to create international cooperation and toward ever more bloated "defense" budgets. The missionary zeal of the "rules-based international order" demands nothing less than unconditional surrender and renders diplomacy a dead letter. This outlook threatens prolonged conventional war and, at worst, a nuclear exchange—the ultimate climate catastrophe.

For decades, until quite recently, Americans became as forgetful of nuclear war as they were of ecological catastrophe. Now nuclear war is being normalized again by politicians calmly discussing nuclear weapons as if they were weapons like any other —as well as by the city of New York, which in a recent public service announcement tells us to get inside, take a shower, and wait for instruction from "officials" after a nuclear attack. For anyone who remembers the absurd Civil Defense drills of the 1950s and '60s, this is a cruel joke. But at least there was diplomacy then.

The normalization of nuclear war is a symptom of the wider war fever that grips elites on both sides of the Atlantic. We cannot think clearly about Soper's inspiriting vision until that fever breaks.

THE ABUNDANCE AGENDA
Will Rinehart

KATE SOPER'S RECENT WORK, showcased in this essay and in her book *Post-Growth Living* (2020), explores the fundamental question of Western philosophy, but constrained by the central political problem of our time: What does the good life look like in the face of climate change?

According to Soper, we need a new kind of politics that challenges the "stranglehold of the work ethic on the Western way of life" and that embraces a world where "work and income are more fairly distributed, coparenting and part-time work become the norm, and everyone has the means and time for sustainable forms of activity and life-enhancement." Rather than providing the exact political response, Soper explores the conditions that the new political response should meet. She asks the reader to figure out how to get there.

Soper is on the right path in questioning the assumption "that more sustainable consumption will always involve sacrifice rather than improve well-being." But she doesn't go far enough. The only framework that checks off all the boxes of her vision for society is a politics rooted in abundance.

If, as Soper says, we want to "transform urban and rural living, especially for children, and provide more tranquil space for reflection" as well as create "more sustainable ways of living and working," then cities will have to be rebuilt densely. In other words, we need *abundant housing* and *cheaper infrastructure*. If we are going to tackle climate change, energy and industry are going to need to undergo decarbonization, and then after that project is done, carbon will need to be pulled from air. In other words, we are going to need *abundant green energy*. And Soper's imagined future is a world of *personal abundance*, where jobs, education, and investment are sufficiently plentiful to empower people to exert more control over how and what they spend their days on.

How can we get there? We must be honest about the constraints we face with climate change. Fortunately, it is not all bad news. For one thing, the worst-case scenarios David Wallace-Wells laid out in *The Uninhabitable Earth* (2019) now seem unlikely. As he detailed last year, a lot has changed: "Thanks to the rapid death of coal, the revolution in the price of renewable energy, and a global climate politics forged by a generational awakening, the expectation is for about three degrees [Celsius]" of warming.

While our future will be filled with heat, climate related disruptions, and higher costs, Wallace-Wells and others are now optimistic that change is possible. The prices for solar and wind have dropped. Many companies, large and small, have made climate commitments to reduce their emissions. Nuclear is back on the table. The wrangling in the U.S. Senate over the climate bill aside, a lot of decarbonization has happened in the absence of comprehensive national rules.

But even if the United States electorate were to prioritize climate issues and implement a grand plan, more would be needed. Keeping the world to two degrees of warming could only happen if 10 billion metric tons of carbon were removed each year by 2050. Then, every year after that, 20 billion metric tons will need to be pulled annually. All of the plans *assume* decarbonization. The future will need to be a world with negative emissions technologies deployed at scale. Doing less is not enough. We have to do more, and we have to do it better.

The United States is emerging from COVID-19 with changed circumstances. The switch to renewables in the past decade has proven that real movement on climate is possible. Meanwhile, the pandemic showed that innovation can happen quickly, with vaccines designed and produced at record speed. So there are good reasons to be optimistic that we can do dramatically better in the future.

The politics coming from this crucible is one born of a new mindset. It's about building smarter, cheaper, and better. Ezra Klein calls it "supply-side progressivism." Noah Smith calls it a "new industrialism." The *Atlantic*'s Derek Thompson and my colleague Eli Dourado call it "the abundance agenda." At least for now, this vision offers the most realistic path to a sustainable future because it forces policies to be focused on constraints. There is only one means of reducing constraints, and it is through abundance.

This isn't an agenda of degrowth, but a reframing of what growth should achieve. As Thompson explains, "The abundance agenda aims for growth, not because growth is an end but because it is the best means to achieve the ends that we care about: more comfortable lives, with more power to do what we want, with more time devoted to what we love." Soper is right to chide crass consumerism, but we must be clear-eyed about current scarcity of key goods and products. Sources of renewable energy are only the start.

Abundance is a big tent because a lot of changes are needed. We need abundance in housing, infrastructure, medicine, education, and well-paying jobs. Achieving the abundance agenda will mean the development of clean geothermal energy and next-generation nuclear. Dense housing needs to be built, the electrical grid needs upgrading, airports need investment, and a huge range of environmental projects need to be pursued. There is a lot of work to be done to give all people the resources for a good life.

Soper is right that a political response is needed, and her intuition is correct that we shouldn't pull back on technology. More sustainable consumption—the world that we all want—doesn't have to involve sacrifice. It is going to require an overhaul. Above all, we need to build.

DEGROWTH IS A DISTRACTION
Jayati Ghosh

KATE SOPER MAKES an excellent critique of the obsession with consumerist gratification that is so widespread in rich capitalist countries (and, increasingly, among the rich in poorer countries). In this way, consumerism indeed serves as the lifeblood of contemporary capitalism. I completely agree with her point that "the overall aim must be to wrest control of global wealth and material resources from the grip—and accompanying ecological dereliction—of a relatively small corporate elite."

There is no doubt, as I have written elsewhere, that GDP is a terrible indicator of human progress or even of material well-being. I believe that this is something that both those who argue for "green growth" and those who insist on the need for "degrowth" are agreed upon. All of us are concerned with achieving an economy that delivers our desired social goals: health for all; the ability to provide basic needs and develop human capabilities for everyone; the universal ability to contribute to and benefit from society; and living in harmony with nature and the planet.

The main barrier to achieving these goals is obviously the continuing power of big capital and its influence in state policies, aided by a short-termist approach that fails to even recognize the immediate dangers of ecological tipping points. Humanity is hurtling toward environmental, planetary, and social disaster, and patriarchal finance capitalism is our common enemy.

Economic and social strategies of both "green growth" and "degrowth" share this view, and they advocate similar if not identical economic and social strategies. So why should we obsess about whether GDP rises or falls as these strategies are implemented? What matters is the pattern of economic activity and the distribution of its gains. In some countries GDP might rise, and in others it might fall; these changes would be byproducts, ideally irrelevant ones. Insisting on degrowth is a distraction—probably a hugely counterproductive one—because it misses the point and alienates many potential allies.

Soper's concerns about "presentism" and the need to consider previous forms of economic organization could well be justified. Awareness of past social orientations and ongoing efforts to revive them and implement their insights in some form are important. For example, the Quichua notion of *Sumak Kawsay*, which has been translated as *buen vivir* or living well, more correctly describes "a life with dignity, plenitude, balance, and harmony." Ideas like *Ubuntu* in Africa and *Swaraj* in India also emphasize not just social cohesion but also harmony with nature.

But we should not romanticize life in the past, which in much of the world, until quite recently, could still be characterized, in Thomas Hobbes's formulation, as "poor, nasty, brutish, and short." In the long course of human history, one of the most striking features of the twentieth century—simultaneously a terrible time in many ways and for many people—was the dramatic increase in life expectancy in *all* the regions of the world. After around two millennia when average life expectancy is estimated to have remained broadly flat at around twenty-eight to thirty-two years, it started increasing in the nineteenth century in today's rich (then, colonizing) countries. Over the twentieth century the average of world life expectancy doubled—and the gains were spread across countries. What is more, the gaps between countries, though still very large, have reduced since 1950. Max Roser notes that "today most people in the world can expect to live as long as those in the very richest countries in 1950."

This historically remarkable change reflects major improvements in health: mostly (but not only) declining child and maternal mortality, improved nutrition, and containment of several infectious diseases. This is real human progress, which should not be discounted.

If Soper thinks too well of the past, she also says too little about inequality. She accepts that "economic growth will be needed in the short term to ensure the provision of basic needs in the poorest nations." But many of Soper's arguments apply only to the rich in the wealthiest countries, and especially the top 10 percent and richest 1 percent of the income distribution, whose carbon emissions have skyrocketed in the past two decades. They also apply to the top 10 percent and 1 percent of the rest of the world, which has also shown rapidly increasing carbon emissions. But work done by Lucas Chancel of the World Inequality Lab shows that per capita emissions from low- and middle-income groups in rich countries declined between 1990 and 2019. Since emissions are a reasonable proxy for other resource use as well, the data suggests that the very rich globally, not the rest of the society even in rich countries, are to blame for overconsumption.

Soper is right that consumerist aspirations are encouraged and even instigated by a global capitalist system designed to profit from them. But consumerism is not the only route to higher incomes. They also arise in the process of meeting minimum basic needs—those necessary to live with dignity and develop one's human capability. For the greater part of the world's population, these goals are still far away. A forthcoming book, *Earth for All*, from the Transformational Economics Commission of the Club of Rome (of which I am a member), highlights that only at income levels around $15,000 per capita could we create conditions necessary to achieve the UN's Sustainable Development Goals. Incomes in about a hundred countries—many with large populations—fall well below that level. Increasing them would require not just time but a reversal of many of the current features of the global economic architecture and its economic power imbalances.

From a global perspective, then, some of Soper's recommendations, while possibly applicable to many economic and social activities in rich countries, ring a little false. Capitalism surely drives people to work excessively and creates desires and fragilities that force them to work, but peasants across much of the world would find the idea of reducing the workweek laughable: nature does not allow for such luxury. And the unpaid women care workers across the world also cannot decide, in the absence of alternatives, simply to avoid such work or reduce the time they allocate to it.

No doubt Soper recognizes all this, and I am in complete agreement with her plea for "a politics of prosperity that dissociates pleasure and fulfilment from resource-intensive consumption." I would simply argue for a more nuanced interpretation of that vision—one that takes into account the existence of sharp inequalities, looks at broader social goals for the economy rather than focusing on GDP, and takes seriously her own call to "to avoid fanciful assumptions about what would constitute globally sustainable forms of industry and lifestyle."

A BOURGEOIS REVOLUTION
Nanjala Nyabola

CAN A BOURGEOIS REVOLUTION save the world?

In 2017 I spent a few days covering the drought in Lodwar, the largest town in Turkana County, Kenya, and one of the poorest regions in the world. Goats, perhaps the hardiest domesticated animal, were dying because there was simply no pasture left; they had taken to eating poisonous plants and plastic waste. As farmers at the market told me their stories of loss, I noticed the plastic all around us—wrapped around acacia thorns in the trees and blowing down the dusty road like some kind of modern tumbleweed. I had seen similar images in the capital of Somaliland, where they call the multicolored plastic bags rustling in the trees "the flowers of Hargeisa." No matter how difficult it was for food and water to make its way to the driest corners of the continent, somehow plastic found a way.

As I read Kate Soper's essay, I kept imagining how the people of Turkana would respond to it. Not that a theory or a proposal must be universally applicable. Rather, I wondered whether her ideas could be translated into fundamentally different contexts, or at least received by a very different audience than she appears to imagine. I fear they cannot, and that ultimately Soper's essay does not see or speak to the whole globe.

To be sure, Soper begins by lamenting that the "consumer culture [capitalist production] has bequeathed is often accepted as if it were a natural legacy to be preserved as far as possible." Like her, I regret how "mainstream politics . . . remains dominated by narrow disputes" that take a capitalist paradigm of development for granted (even under "green growth") and that fail to "entertain other ideas of progress and prosperity." And I firmly agree we should look to "societies with traditions of less industrialized but more sustainable methods of production and modes of consuming."

But rather than make good on this prescription, Soper simply forsakes it. Instead she speaks to "concerned consumers in more affluent societies," who she claims "must lead the way" in imagining "a more viable, enjoyable future." And even then, the major obligation she appears to think such people have toward the rest of the world is making different lifestyle choices—not, say, forging a revolutionary movement against capitalism, in solidarity with (if not led by) the more sustainable societies she mentions in passing. This is not even a call for a bourgeois *revolution*. It is an exercise in bourgeois moralism.

Instead, I think that the critique of capitalism with which Soper begins must take precedence over calls for an "alternative hedonism" in rich countries. The crisis of the current model of development will not be mitigated simply by people in wealthy countries regulating their relationship with stuff. Certainly, it is necessary for the bourgeoisie in wealthy countries to change their patterns of consumption in order to address the perils of climate change. But there has to be a fundamental shift in the role that material goods play in our lives.

The solution is not just to work less, or to consume less. The solution is to completely gut the paradigm of what it means to exist in a shared world and begin again. Labor must be revolutionized, not merely reorganized. In short, we must completely reorient human experience away from consumption and toward harmony—not just toward equilibrium but restoration of the natural world that has been devastated so completely. The Turkana drought was caused by climate change, but the region won't be restored by carbon credits or trading harm. The crisis will only be solved by more countries getting off the treadmill altogether.

As Soper suggests at the outset, the heart of the issue is the social construct of wealth. In capitalist societies wealth is measured by money, and more specifically by the amount of money one is able to hoard either in a bank or in assets. Making more money than you can feasibly spend in a lifetime is celebrated as success, and having a critical mass of wealth hoarders within a nation's borders is considered good economic planning. But wealth is not just money; it is what money makes possible. Today wealth unfortunately stands for the opportunities and the perspectives accorded to those who have money, the diffidence afforded to people who have money because of what they are believed to be capable of. Wealth is the abstract measure of possibility.

There are still societies in the world in which wealth is not measured directly through money. In some communities in Kenya, for example, wealth is still measured by the size of one's family, so people with larger families are given a certain moral cache or authority. This is independent of the ability to provide for these children, in part because it presumes a synergy with the natural world and the environment. The presumption is that if the children survived childhood then they were meant to be here, and the world will provide for them. This view clashes crudely with the money-driven society—where schools charge tuition, and nutritious food beyond what can grow near the homestead or be harvested nearby costs money. Of course, this perspective also instrumentalizes women's bodies in toxic ways. But the underlying ethos is distinct: money is not the weight that tips the scales one way or the other to determine whether a person is wealthy.

For too many people, wealth is a fetish. Their lives are primarily organized around acquiring and maintaining it, and this scales up to the national level. Minority communities are taught that wealth is freedom. A country is considered successful when it can deliver wealth—not peace, justice, or equality. In this way even opposition to the reigning model of development can reinforce it. In countries that have no social safety net, the absence of wealth directly results in the absence of the basics—food, shelter, clothing, education, health care. In poor countries, wealth is insulation against having to see a government doctor at an under-resourced clinic, for example. When I was backpacking through a village in Togo in 2007, I had to see a doctor, but there were no private clinics around. When I went to the government clinic to get a blood test, I was given a choice between a rusted scalpel to which a piece of cotton had been stuck or a trip down to the corner shop to buy a razor. Of course, I chose the walk to the shop, but the idea that someone could walk into that clinic and not have that buffer of choice has stayed with me for fifteen years.

The people of this village aren't poor because they lack money. They are poor because money has been inserted as an obstacle to achieving the basics of a decent life. Poverty, or the lack of wealth, is not about the lack of money but the lack of access to what money represents. It is the lack of that abstract possibility that money makes possible.

This is the more fundamental issue that unites all the propositions of Soper's argument. The problem we face can't be solved by nibbling at lifestyle questions. It requires the deeper philosophical engagement with what it means to live and be in the world—as well as who counts within it—that Soper gestures at but ultimately relegates to the margin. A bourgeois revolution might delay the inevitable, but unless we revolutionize the role that money plays in our societies—unless we confront the wealth fetish that divides the deserving from undeserving—we will merely be kicking the can down the road.

FINAL RESPONSE
Kate Soper

I APPRECIATE the generous, astute responses and thank their authors. They draw attention to some of the biggest questions about what policy will be needed to direct the general remaking of the global order, and as such defy quick, easy answers. Some of their questions are addressed more fully in my book *Post-Growth Living: For an Alternative Hedonism* (2020), notably issues relating to inequality and the rationale for my focus on affluent consumption. In the space I have here, I'll reply as succinctly as I can to the most crucial issues that were raised.

In Robert Pollin's advocacy of the Green New Deal, as well as in Will Rinehart's defense of what he terms "the abundance agenda," the major issue is raised about the role of "growth" in delivering a green renaissance. Jayati Ghosh also addresses this, albeit more circumspectly, with her advice against obsessing over GDP. I agree with Pollin that degrowth within an unrevised capitalist economy is disastrous for the majority, and may not do much to reduce carbon emissions. I also accept that in any transition beyond that economy, growth will be needed in key areas of industry and social provision.

The central question, however, concerns its conceptual status within any economic argument on the future. Are we viewing "growth" in some areas (renewable energy, housing provision, education, and caring services, for example) as needed forms of productive expansion within an economic system that is being redesigned in order to foster ways of living very different from those of profit-driven, capitalist consumer culture? Or are we viewing "growth" as an essential and permanent dynamic of any effective economic order, and thus as both compatible with environmental conservation and enduringly sustainable? If the latter, I, along with a growing number of economists, reject it, and would cite in support the many studies exposing the folly of thinking that growth is consistent with conservation (see, for example, the 2019 "Decoupling Debunked" report from the European Environmental Bureau, and a similarly damning verdict in the same year from the European Environmental Agency). Indeed, it is not those who support the degrowth transition who have to prove the wisdom of their case, but those committed to a decoupling project for which to date there is no evidence.

In line with this, while I certainly accept Rinehart's point that the required level of decarbonization is daunting, my concern is how we build political enthusiasm for the changes of lifestyle it will require. One way we might do so, I suggest, is to place greater emphasis on the gratifications that would follow—for us and all future generations—from a radical break with consumerism.

Pollin and Rinehart, by contrast, present the "greened" economy as continuing to deliver capitalist-influenced ways of living (flying, driving, full employment)—and this is maybe also implicit in some of the other comments. That avoids really engaging with my argument for alternative hedonism, which questions not only the enduring ecological viability of that degree of "business as usual," but also the presumption that it serves a "natural" way of life that we (all of us?) shall always want and seek to preserve. Pollin, for example, speaks of raising "mass living standards." I am asking, among other questions, what we might understand by the phrase, and whether we might want to rethink these "standards" in the light of ecological breakdown. So, yes, I support workers caught in the transition from the fossil fuel economy—but I would like us to do so within a context of promoting a less work-centered, growth-driven view of economic health. On this point, Pollin is right to challenge me on the role of unions: I should have noted (as, indeed, I do in my book) that some are now incorporating greener policies. A few even advocate a shorter working week—a move that would help to reduce energy and resource use *and* allow for more free time and personal autonomy.

As indicated here, I do not subscribe to Ghosh's view that "green growth" and "degrowth" endorse "similar, if not identical, policies." But she and Nanjala Nyabola are quite right to draw attention to the stark inequalities of the current global order, and to the immense disparities between richer and poorer nations and peoples in their respective contributions to environmental degradation. I completely agree with Ghosh on the priority that needs to be given to providing the means for a decent, dignified life to the 80 percent of the global community currently deprived of them.

If I seem—mistakenly, in the view of both Ghosh and Nyabola —to focus too exclusively on the most affluent minority, it is precisely because it is their consumption that is most accountable for environmental collapse, and they whom I view as most needing to take the lead in shifting to more sustainable ways of living. Nyabola charges me with not speaking "to the whole world" and contrasts my "nibbling with lifestyle questions" with her own call for a revolutionary movement against capitalism. But the fundamental question for me is one of agency: Who is to begin to forge that revolution, and can it be set in motion without significant support from those resisting the consumerist way of living within the richest nations?

My hope is that, by altering conceptions of self-interest among the most affluent, alternative hedonism could help to set off a relay of political pressures for creating a fairer and sustainable global order. It might also contribute to the critique of neocolonial "development" orthodoxy. In this critique, past ways of living and working should not be romanticized, but nor should the unsustainable and vandalizing consumerism of the richest nations be glamorized as any kind of model for the future.

Western affluence has delivered benefits for health and longevity, but it can no longer be allowed to dominate ideas of progress and well-being. Globally now, we need to look to other sources to shape a "politics of prosperity" for the future—whether it be past methods of provisioning, the knowledge and experiences of poorer nations and marginalized communities, or the less growth-driven imaginings of thinkers, technicians, and cultural workers, wherever they are to be found. Its priority will not be to secure ways for the more privileged to continue to fly and drive as before. But it also cannot be achieved by abstracting from consumption and simply advocating "harmony," since consumption is essential to the meeting of even the most basic needs. I share much of Nyabola's despair over the fetish of money and its dominant role in defining value. But I am aware, too, that were we to be rid of that role and to move to something more akin to Marx's "second-stage socialism" of "distribution according to need," we would still need agreement on what we mean by "prospering," and on what is to count as "need." Money is a curse. But to dispense with it is not to dispense with politics.

I agree with Lida Maxwell that capitalist ideology seeks to persuade people that poverty is self-induced rather than the outcome of exploitative relations. I am happy, too, to go along with her general point that we should conceive of desire not as lack but as "fullness" (although I am not sure I have entirely understood what is meant by that). Certainly, I myself am speaking to an alternative view of desire and its aspirations. In particular, I am trying to strengthen the bridge between the disaffection people so frequently voice about the most visible effects of affluent consumption— stress, ill health, time scarcity, pollution, waste—and an explicit politics of degrowth. And, yes, I conceive of alternative hedonism and its associated desires as directing attention to collective conditions and political structures. The promotion of a less individualized consumption and a more citizenly, community-oriented understanding of pleasure is central to its outlook.

Last but not least, I am grateful to Jackson Lears for his stimulating comment, on two main counts. First, Lears provides an insightful historical survey of the reasons underlying the post-1970s dissolution, in both eco-writing and campaigning, of the linkage between environmental conservation, improved happiness, and human well-being. I had not much thought about this disappearance, but find his reflections on this, and on the resurgence of an associated "technophilia," interesting and persuasive.

Second, I am grateful to him for noting the brevity and inadequacy of my mention of the war in Ukraine. This was due in part to the war still being in its earliest days when I penned the article, but Lears is certainly right to draw attention to the fearsome impact of the continuing hostilities in "normalizing" nuclear war, drumming up a war fever on both sides of the Atlantic, and eroding international cooperation on the environment. As someone who has been an active campaigner for nuclear disarmament (especially during the 1980s with the European Nuclear Disarmament movement), his remarks strike a chord. The current situation at Zaporizhzhia should give pause to those arguing for more nuclear reactors as a path toward global greening. I look with horror on the current standoff between the major powers, which brings back all the terrors of the Cold War—but, as Lears says, made more terrible because of the absence of diplomacy, and because of the ignorant, gung-ho attitudes of several of those with fingers on or near the button.

My fear has always been that, in the absence of the needed economic and political changes, climate-induced migration and global competition over resources (including livable space) will precipitate major conflict—possibly nuclear, in which case almost certainly terminal—well before global warming in itself sets us on the path to extinction. The war in Ukraine—which itself must be viewed in the context of Kremlin alarm over net-zero carbon policies, given Russian economic reliance on gas and oil exports—has greatly increased that risk.

ESSAYS

ESSAYS

THE ORDINARY PLEASURES OF BLACK MOTHERHOOD

Jennifer C. Nash

WHEN MY PARENTS MOVED to Chapel Hill, North Carolina, they carried their inheritance with them: tattered photo albums whose adhesive had given way and envelopes bursting with fading pictures of the faces of relatives whose names we no longer know. One of my pandemic pastimes became sifting through this vast collection of family photographs.

There are pictures of my mother's family: my grandfather's stint in the Navy, my grandmother teaching elementary school students. There are pictures of my mother and her parents traveling across the country, portraits of a Black middle-class family who had a desire to see the world. My grandfather meticulously labeled his blurry pictures of Niagara Falls, the Golden Gate Bridge, Harvard's Widener Library.

There are far fewer pictures of my father's family. My father's childhood was marked by my grandfather's sudden cancer diagnosis, which launched my father into an early adulthood working in a zipper factory and a candy store. My father became indoctrinated into a set of habits that have shaped his life ever since: He clips coupons. He only buys things that are on sale. He will drive an extra ten minutes to save a fraction of a dollar on gas. He moves through the world with a sense that everything can change on a dime.

As a relief from pandemic teaching, sorting pictures promised a form of mindless labor. I also welcomed the chance to hold the past—to literally touch it, to engage in the practice of what Black feminist legal scholar Patricia J. Williams calls "gathering the ghosts." As I mother, and as I watch my own mother fade, I am hungry to collect stories of the past, to share them with my daughter so she can hold them and do whatever she pleases with them, including freeing herself from them. She will have to forge her own relationship to her history, to the people who have come before her. But I want her to at least see these pictures, to know that there are predilections, interests, investments, and ways of being in the world that are not just hers, that come from the people before us.

I am a great documentarian of my daughter's life. I have a picture of nearly every day of her six years of existence. I have videos of her learning how to walk, negotiating her way out of potty training, and reading Bill Martin and Eric Carle's *Brown Bear, Brown Bear, What Do You See?* (1967). I know what she looked like on this day two years ago, three years ago, and four years ago. Thanks to my iPhone, my digital archive of her life is expansive, and greatly oriented toward the ordinary. But my family's photographs are different. They were shot on film, and they are records of an event, even if the event was posing for the picture. There are images of parties and holidays, but few pictures of a new haircut, the clouds as a rainstorm rolled in, a half-eaten breakfast arranged on a plate.

My daughter is part of an archived generation. She can remember pictures of events more than she can remember the actual events. She might not remember watching wet snowflakes slap against the glass of our apartment in Chicago, but she has seen the video, and it has taken the place of memory. I don't yet know what it will mean for her to narrate the story of herself when she has so much visual evidence of who she was. I piece together my family's story from lack—the scant images that are preserved. My daughter will have to piece together her story from abundance.

MY MOST RECENT BOOK, *Birthing Black Mothers* (2021), was born in a delivery room in Rockville, Maryland, in precisely the moment when my daughter—a sticky screaming mass—was placed on my chest and I whispered to her, "Welcome to the world, it's nice to meet you." Ever since, I have devoted my research to Black mothers: Black mothers dying in hospitals; Black infants and their precarity; Black mothers and babies navigating institutional medical spaces like pediatricians' offices. I think about the current infant formula crisis and its effects on Black infants and their mothers, who are less likely to breastfeed than other parents. And I track how politicians have made Black maternal health a talking point, a left credential, with little attention paid to Black mothers' actual varied, heterogeneous needs and desires.

As I have researched the death worlds that swirl around Black mothers, I have also mothered. I have mothered as a Black feminist, which means that I have done it—or hoped to do it—with a sense that mothering is about a commitment to relationality and coexistence, sometimes peaceable and sometimes fraught, always alive and dynamic. I have devoted my intellectual life to Black feminist theory, a tradition that informs how I think about nearly everything. It has taught me to approach mothering as a project of living alongside another being who is, in her earliest years, far more vulnerable than I am. What might it mean, this tradition demands that I ask, to imagine the world as capable of caring for the most vulnerable? To *insist* that the world care for the most vulnerable?

As a Black feminist, mother, and scholar who is weary of how the academic (and political) world treats "racial and gender alterity" as, in literary scholar Ann duCille's words, little more than "a hot commodity," I am tired. I read—and write about—Black thinkers who claim Black mothering as a revolutionary act, as a radical practice of making a world to protect Black life. I come to this work keenly aware of how women's work remains undervalued and invisible—of how thanking women for that work often takes the place of acknowledging the debt owed for it. The pandemic has made clearer than ever how care work is both essential and demonized. We need care; those who provide it are among the least respected in our society.

I don't see my mothering practices as resistant, revolutionary, or romantic, nor do I want to see them as such. I am not invested in having my choice to prepare eggplant or grilled cheese read as a radical one or even as a political one. Instead, I am interested in the ordinary pleasures of watching my daughter grow. Yet a desire for a world where she—and the friends she holds dear—can grow, live, and breathe *is* a political one, a claim that has to be asserted in a world motivated by a death drive that has never been more visible.

I would like to live in a world in which Black mothers do not only come into view as political parables of pathology or resilience. I want space for the Black ordinary. Black feminist scholars and activists have often been animated by a single question: What does freedom look like? The Black ordinary is one form of freedom. As a Black mother, this means a world where how I parent—the choices I make about the most seemingly ordinary aspects of daily life—are simply mundane rather than overburdened with meaning. I want to move through the world without the sense that political symbolism is carried on my back.

My daughter is six years old. She has just finished kindergarten, survived a second year of pandemic schooling, and, somehow, in the midst of the brokenness of the world, she has become more herself: a reader, a dancer, a committed friend, a lover of cucumber and avocado rolls, a pen pal, a jokester. I have watched her face become more like mine. I recognize the moments when I see her look back at me with my own dark eyes, and when I see my mother's face appear on her face. In those moments, I think—*feel*, even—the histories that bind us, even the ones we don't know yet, the ones each generation of our family has had to lose and discover, find and tell again. I think of Williams channeling novelist Ruth Ozeki: "What did your face look like before your parents were born?"

BLACK MOTHERS ARE DYING in disproportionate numbers. I am surrounded by articles that document how the pandemic has intensified the Black maternal mortality crisis. My own Black mother is dying, slowly. She has Alzheimer's, and I experience it as loss in slow motion.

All around me is evidence of how she is slowly fading. All around me is an archive of loss.

But this is not a eulogy. It's about a set of conditions that made it possible for us—my parents, my husband, my daughter, and I—to live in the same place, that have made possible what is perhaps the biggest pleasure of my life: Sunday dinner. I never cooked before the pandemic. But with a small child suddenly at home full-time, and the anxiety, grief, and tedium of the early days of the pandemic bearing down on us, I turned my attention to food preparation. This survival strategy has become a habit, and a way of making tangible my desire to care for my parents.

Every Sunday, when my mother finishes her meal, she abruptly stands. She grabs plates from the table and walks them into the kitchen. She never lingers at the dinner table for conversation or small talk. Instead, we hear the water running, the scrubbing of the sponges against pots and pans. She hums as she works—humming has become her constant companion as her memory has faded. My mother and I talk less and less now—she has fewer words—but when I hear her standing in the kitchen scrubbing vigorously, I feel her desire to still give me something, to find a way to keep mothering me through the fog of searching for the right words.

I send my parents home with plastic containers full of food. Every Sunday when they come over, they return the empty boxes. Our weeks are marked by this choreography: filling and emptying boxes. I joke that the motto of parenting is, *Wash, dry, repeat.* There is a rhythm—sometimes relentless, sometimes comforting—to life with a still-small child. There is a rhythm—sometimes relentless, sometimes comforting—to life with aging parents. I cook, I feed them, my mother scrapes our plates and cleans our kitchen: *Wash, dry, repeat.*

I often tell my daughter—not in the register of the morbid, but in the register of something I can only call truth—that what we have now is not permanent. I remind her, though I know she is too young to fully understand it, that the world we have now, where my parents join us each Sunday for dinner, is fragile. I tell her that one day, they might not be able to do it, or they might not be able to do it together. I see her imagining my father coming to our house without my mother. We have had exactly two moments where he has come to our house without her, and we have all found it dizzying. None of us name it as such, but we share the strange sense of what might come. My mother is already not entirely with us, not as she used to be. But the idea of her wholly absent is unbearable. It is agonizing to say all of this to a six-year-old. It is utterly necessary to say it to her.

Last night, my daughter and I sat next to each other sorting family pictures. We made two piles: old and very old. My daughter held up a picture of my mother in which her animated face is caught mid-laugh. She said, "Grandma's smile looks the same as now." I want her to know that our routine is as fragile as that smile. I want her to know that my mother's smile over Sunday dinner is its own delicate and profound pleasure, that it will not last no matter how desperately we want it to. I want her to know that we might not name this as pleasure right now, we might only call it Sunday dinner, as the way we begin each week, as ordinary as dicing onions and marinating salmon, as ordinary as the sound of a sponge scrubbing the bottom of a pan.

JUST WEAR YOUR SMILE: THE GENDER POLITICS OF POSITIVE PSYCHOLOGY

Micki McElya

You'll have the boys a-lining up single file
If you just wear your smile.
Cass Elliot, "When I Just Wear My Smile" (1969)

AS MASK MANDATES eased across the United States, many women bemoaned the inevitable return of one of the more insidious banalities of misogyny: men telling them to smile. COVID-19 masking had offered a kind of consciousness-raising for many women, the absence of the requirement to smile in public making stark their habitual, constant emotional labor. One woman told a reporter for the *Daily Beast*, "Best thing about the masks is that men can't tell me to smile when I'm out in public." Another said she planned to continue wearing masks despite changes to the rules in her community, because "it's just so nice and freeing to be able to decide whether to smile or not, just based on how I feel personally."

These women's comments were reminiscent of remarks made by Women's Liberation activist Shulamith Firestone, who explained in her foundational 1970 book *The Dialectic of Sex*: "My 'dream' action for the women's liberation movement: *a smile boycott*, at which declaration all women would instantly abandon their 'pleasing' smiles, henceforth smiling only when something pleased *them*." Firestone's use of the term "pleasing" remains machete-sharp, slicing through both sides of the compulsory smile interaction. A woman is "pleasing" to look at because she is smiling, and she is "pleasing" the man because he expects her to. At base, Firestone argues, the woman's smile "indicates acquiescence of the victim to her own oppression." And, if a man doesn't get it—on the subway, at work, in the cereal aisle at the grocery store, in class, at a club, walking down the street—he demands it. "You should smile more." "Come on, lady, smile!" "Lighten up!" "You have Resting Bitch Face." "Why are you so angry?" "Your clients/coworkers/boss would find you more approachable if you smiled more." "Smile, bitch!"

Fortunately, our popular culture is finally starting to rally behind the position that men must stop telling women to smile. At the same time, however, a prominent subfield of psychology known as Positive Psychology, which purports to be the science of the good life, continues to insist that people—and especially women—should smile.

In 2001 psychologists LeeAnne Harker and Dacher Keltner published the findings of their study on smiling in the *Journal of Personality and Social Psychology*. The question the study sought to answer was simple: Was it possible to look at women's college yearbook photos and from them make predictions about their future happiness? Yes, the Berkeley psychologists concluded, it was. Their predictions hinged on whether the women were smiling. But not just smiling; they had to be giving the camera (and the photographer behind it) an authentic smile—what supermodel Tyra Banks would call a "smize," a smile that reaches the eyes. This "true" smile, the researchers contended, indicated that the subject was experiencing positive emotions like happiness or joy. And what proved that these smiling women went on to experience lives of true happiness and well-being? In addition to their self-reports, the women hadn't stayed single beyond the age of twenty-seven and had divorce-free marriages.

This all may seem self-evidently ridiculous, or at least very far down on a list of the world's current problems, but this study—and the research movement it emerged from—have serious repercussions. Positive Psychology remains a leading school of thought in academic psychology, clinical therapy, management and organizational consulting, and coaching. With its interdisciplinary bedfellow Happiness Studies, Positive Psychology represents a large share of self-help books released every year, a publishing market worth about $10.5 billion in the United States in 2020, which itself represents only a small sliver of the billions generated annually by the global mental wellness industry. Since November 2008, luminaries of Positive Psychology, including its founder Martin E.P. Seligman, have worked with the U.S. Army to implement service-wide resilience training, despite a lack of evidence that the program offers soldiers any benefit. Other initiatives run by the field's disciples stretch into health care, education, law, policing, human resources, international relief, and design. In short, tens of millions of people around the world are impacted directly by Positive Psychology. It matters, then, that we ask how it gave birth to such a seemingly unscientific idea as a "true" smile, and through that inquiry consider how its patriarchal assumptions of what constitutes "happiness" came to be enshrined in the science of psychology.

Fair warning: like so many stories of misogyny, the tale involves a hot tub.

POSITIVE PSYCHOLOGY'S OFFICIAL HISTORY is a Great Man story. It begins in 1998 when University of Pennsylvania psychologist Martin E.P. Seligman gave his inaugural address as the new president of the American Psychological Association, "Building Human Strength: Psychology's Forgotten Mission." He argued that since World War II, the field had become too narrowly focused on mental illness and suffering; as well, it had been "sidetracked" by the priorities of research funders, including the insurance and pharmaceutical industries. As president of the APA, he was announcing a new set of priorities "to reorient psychology to its two neglected missions, making normal people stronger and more productive as well as making high human potential actual." Seligman called the new field to be guided by these concerns "Positive Psychology."

Now just two decades in, Positive Psychology has claimed significant conceptual and research space in the wider disciplinary worlds of psychology and academic social science generally, especially economics. Psychologists in the field have become the go-to consultants for governmental health care agencies, militaries, police, NGOs, and corporations. But Positive Psychology has also garnered substantial criticism, and not only for its imperious claims to novelty (Albert Maslow, of "hierarchy of needs" fame, had called for "a Positive Psychology" in his 1954 book *Motivation and Personality*). Critics of Positive Psychology note how it embraces a neoliberal logic that shifts the onus of unhappiness and inequality away from larger systems onto individual behavior, making sadness a matter of "mindset," personal responsibility, and choice. Positive Psychology lends the language and authority of "science"—"data," "evidence-based," "universal," "fact"—to a highly subjective and ideologically driven version of what constitutes common values, individual strengths, and a good life. In the end, critics charge, its ultimate aim is to assimilate people at their deepest levels to the inequities, oppression, stress, and thwarted aspirations of neoliberal capitalism, privatization, austerity, and the gig economy.

Less well-explored have been the field's insidious assumptions that happiness and well-being are fundamentally tied to normative gender roles, heterosexual monogamy, family values, Christian ethics, white supremacy, American exceptionalism, and militarism. With the end of "Don't Ask, Don't Tell" and the legalization of same-sex marriage, this has been expanded to include homonormative marriage and some gays' and lesbians' military service.

None of this is surprising if one considers who joined Seligman in the Caymans in 1998 for Positive Psychology's grand strategy launch meeting. In his recent memoir, *The Hope Circuit: A Psychologist's Journey from Helplessness to Optimism* (2018), Seligman paints a remarkable picture of the new subfield's founding moments. He describes two different private funders reaching out to him with offers of financial support to develop Positive Psychology after his inaugural APA speech. The first was the chairman of opinion poll company Gallup, Inc., Donald Clifton. Clifton had been a professor of educational psychology before leaving academia in the late 1960s to start a personnel selection firm that pioneered the use of personality testing in hiring. The second was John Templeton, Jr., on behalf of the John Templeton Foundation and his father, a billionaire investor-turned-philanthropist looking to support work probing the "big questions" arising at the intersections of science and religion.

Clifton offered Seligman the use of his vacation home (and its hot tub) on Grand Cayman Island for a working group meeting of "the best people in the world to steer positive psychology." This group would include Clifton and Seligman, as well as a number of academic psychologists. These included Mihaly Csikszentmihalyi of "flow" fame; Edward Diener, originator of the concept of "subjective well-being"; Dan Robertson, author of *Aristotle's Psychology* (1999); George Valliant, long-time director of Harvard's longitudinal Study of Adult Development; and a graduate student of Seligman's, Derek Isaacowitz, who was invited to serve as secretary. The group was joined by two scholars from other fields: Kathleen Hall Jamieson, a communications professor specializing in civility and politics and the founding director of the University of Pennsylvania's Annenberg Public Policy Center; and libertarian political philosopher Robert Nozick, best known for his book *Anarchy, State, and Utopia* (1974). As Seligman puts it, "In the huge hot tub outside Don's condo, the cast of characters soaked." Notably, everyone in the hot tub except for the younger Isaacowitz was a white American professor over the age of fifty, and all save Jamieson were men.

The working group agreed upon three research areas falling under Positive Psychology's mission of increasing well-being by "making normal people stronger and more productive." These were "positive experience," "civic fulfillment," and "positive traits." Seligman's elaboration of these resonates with idealized notions of the American Dream and its pursuit of happiness. Positive experiences are "denoted [by] what free people who are not suffering choose" to do and seek. This is supported—civically fulfilled—by "positive institutions that allow for well-being," including "democracy, free press, strong families, and volunteering." Finally, "positive traits" names the personal qualities that make positive experience possible. While there was debate on the matter, Seligman claims that all agreed eventually to the existence of common traits or ways "to think and behave that transcend time and situation" and that Positive Psychology should encourage research on the "universality of goodness."

Over time, this version of universal traits and goodness has incorporated an express argument against cultural relativism, marshalling "evidence-based science" to claim that much of human psychology is universal, only changing at an evolutionary pace. Consequently, Positive Psychology's luminaries insist, there must then also exist universal values, social formations, institutions, and ethics that define what constitutes the good life—and that one can identify with scientific precision what is true, good, and timeless.

DACHER KELTNER AND LEEANNE HARKER began their study of smiling women in 1999, the year that Gallup, Inc., hosted the inaugural Positive Psychology summit at the corporation's headquarters in Lincoln, Nebraska. Harker was a doctoral student; the yearbook smiles study was her dissertation research. Keltner was a newly promoted associate professor of social psychology. He studied positive emotions as evolutionary adaptations that enabled sociality and flourishing in a way similar to the more familiar argument that tendencies toward negative emotionality and cognitions—"negativity bias"— were inherited from early humans who needed constant vigilance to survive. Negativity kept people alive, while positivity made that life worth living. Today, Keltner is a full professor and the founding director of Berkeley's Greater Good Science Center. He is author of several popular books, has appeared in a number of films, hosts the award-winning podcast *The Science of Happiness*, and has served in high-profile consulting positions, including for Google's Empathy Research Lab and the design team at Facebook that created its Reactions feature that replaced the single "Like" button. He also advised Pixar's 2015 blockbuster *Inside Out*.

Since the start of his career in 1989, Keltner has been part of the effort within psychology to shift focus to how positive cognitions and emotionality could counter the effects of negative ones. These efforts, like Positive Psychology, are legacies of North American psychology's disciplinary shift from strict adherence to B. F. Skinner's behaviorism to theories of *cognitive* behavior positing that negative cognitions fuel negative emotions leading to depression, anxiety, and other mental illnesses. In this view, overcoming mental illness hinges on disrupting habitual negative thinking ("cognitive distortions"). The extremely popular treatment modality called Cognitive Behavioral Therapy is perhaps the best-known member of this family tree.

These shifts in psychology accompanied a growing consensus in the field that there exist six primary universal human emotions, identical across cultures and time: Happiness, Surprise, Sadness, Disgust, Anger, and Fear. Alongside these emotions came the identification of the "Big Five" universal dimensions of personality: Extraversion, Agreeableness, Openness, Conscientiousness, and Neuroticism. These claims to fundamental commonalities among humans developed in tandem with simultaneous efforts within and outside of the field to diversify and dismantle the sexism, racism, homophobia, and various cultural ethnocentrisms endemic to experimental and clinical psychology—highlighting the complex entwining of reactionary and liberal impulses to shore up presumptive equations of white, Western, straight, and male with the general category Human, on the one hand, while tethering diversity to assertions that underneath it all everyone is essentially the same.

The positive emotions work of fellow social psychologist Barbara Fredrickson was key to Keltner's own research interests, including his study on yearbook smiles. If Seligman is the "Father of Positive Psychology," as his celebrants claim, Fredrickson is its undisputed mother and a dominant force in the field today. She published her foundational "broaden and build" theory shortly before Seligman's appeal to members of the APA, identifying positive emotions as key to human flourishing.

Positive emotions, she contends, expand or broaden people's senses of their options, leading to more creative actions and solutions. In the deep past, "this served to *build* our ancestors' resources, spurring on their development of assets, abilities, and useful traits," explains Fredrickson in her popular book *Positivity: Groundbreaking Research Reveals How to Embrace the Hidden Strength of Positive Emotions, Overcome Negativity, and Thrive* (2009). The book's subtitle states plainly the meaning of this for people today. Positive emotional expressions are dynamic; they accumulate and propel individuals in an "upward spiral" of growth, happiness, and fulfillment and make them better able to manage and learn from hard times ("post-traumatic growth"). Fredrickson was the only woman invited to present her own research at the Nebraska summit in 1999 and was awarded the inaugural John Templeton Positive Psychology Prize in 2000.

Smiles aren't just indicative or predictive of positive life outcomes, claims Fredrickson, but actually *generate* them. She has applied this theory to everything from faster recovery from the physical manifestations of anger, fear, and sadness to reductions in heart disease, greater cancer survival rates, and living longer with HIV/AIDS. Barbara Ehrenreich, one of Positive Psychology's most trenchant critics, has challenged Positive Psychology's influence on health care in the United States in *Bright Sided: How Positive Thinking is Undermining America* (2009). In the UK, her book was published under the more pointed title: *Smile or Die*.

Although the yearbook smiles study would be celebrated as an early part of the Positive Psychology vanguard, it actually drew upon the very old and contested concept of the "Duchenne

Smile." The moniker was coined in the early 1970s by Paul Ekman, who supervised a young Keltner's postdoc and is credited by many with confirming the existence of basic human emotions signaled by facial expressions common to all—meaning, Ekman claims, they are biological and evolutionary rather than historically contingent cultural forms. This marked a return of sorts to the theories outlined by Charles Darwin in *The Expression of Emotions in Man and Animals* (1872), and even more to the earlier work of Darwin's contemporary, French neurologist Guillaume Duchenne who published *The Mechanism of Human Facial Expression* in 1862. Duchenne's book uses photographs to illustrate how individual muscles of the face move to create different expressions, and classifies what those expressions mean. He innovated the use of what he termed *électrisation localisée*—attaching electrodes to the muscles of the face to manipulate them artificially—a forerunner of today's electrophysiology. It was a painful process for Duchenne's subjects; his book is literally a catalog of tortured expressions.

The smile that would come to bear Duchenne's name a century later is characterized by the motions of two pairs of muscles: the zygomatic majors lifting the cheeks and turning up the corners of the mouth—the motion of an iconic smile—and the orbicularis oculi that squeeze the eyes creating crow's feet at their edges. Without the latter movement, in the French neurologist's taxonomy, one is left with a "fake," unfelt, or merely polite smile. Another element distinguishing the true smile is spontaneity: a fake smile "obeys the will" while an authentic one is "only put into play by the sweet emotions of the soul," Duchenne writes. Ekman, Keltner, and

Fredrickson concur, arguing that the Duchenne smile is a reliable indicator of authentic positive emotion because it cannot be faked.

The central hypothesis of the yearbook smiles study was that "positive emotional expression" indicated by the presence of a Duchenne smile would "predict higher levels of well-being across adulthood." This was premised on the idea that differences in emotional expression relate to stable aspects of personality, traits that remain constant across time and situation. It should follow, the scholars contended, that one instance of positive emotional expression signaled a lifetime of them.

Unlike with many psychology experiments, Keltner and Harker never directly interacted with the subjects of their yearbook smiles study. Rather, all had been participants in the Mills College Longitudinal Study. Run by UC Berkeley's Institute of Personality and Assessment Research (IPAR), it followed graduates of Mills College to track what happened to them throughout adulthood. For their own study, Keltner and Harker examined the Mills women's 1958–60 yearbook photos and compared conclusions about the smiles contained therein with information from the longitudinal study about how their lives had, in their estimation, turned out. Using the Facial Action Coding System (FACS) created by Ekman and a colleague in 1978, Harker and Keltner mapped the expressions of each woman pictured. Of the 114 images they were able to code, all but three of the subjects were smiling. Fifty of the women—just shy of half—were coded as expressing Duchenne smiles.

At no point in their 2001 article do Keltner and Harker offer demographic information for their subjects, beyond sex and average age, despite having this information at hand. Instead, the uniform whiteness and socioeconomic status of the "women" goes unmarked as they are treated as a singular, representative category: the universal Woman. This absence of intersectional understandings gains more meaning when placed in its context: at the same time that Keltner and Harker were writing, the University of California system, and Berkeley in particular, was at the center of national struggles over multicultural education, identity politics, and the dismantling of affirmative action. In short, the psychologists' failure to even remark upon the limitations of their sample is clearly a choice.

The implications of this silence on the part of Keltner and Harker are compounded by the fact that the Mills Longitudinal Study had its own complex relationship to race, gender, and mid-century misogyny. Mills was a small women's college in Oakland, just a few miles away from Berkeley's campus. In the late 1950s, its students were mostly white, well-off if not wealthy, and tended to hail from the new suburban communities sprouting up across California and surrounding states. Betty Friedan would single out Mills as an example of how "women's education" at all but the most elite institutions had been warped into training for housewives.

The Mills Longitudinal Study launched in 1959 with a day-long trip to Berkeley's campus, where—as even Keltner and Harker note—every assessor save for the study's director, Ravenna Helson, was a man. The women spent the entire day with these men and Helson, being interviewed by them and scrutinized as they interacted with their peers and completed personality inventories. From this, the assessors compiled personality profiles of each of the women. Qualities noted in the women's dossiers included whether they "appreciate[d] humor," which Keltner and Harker use as an indicator of positive emotionality in the subjects' day-to-day lives. But the women's files make no note of whether the humor was funny—or, for that matter, how an attempt at humor by a male assessor might have landed in the context of a day that must have felt like the weirdest group blind date ever, complete with an older female chaperone. In a later description of the atmosphere of the day, Keltner could just as well have been describing a school dance when he notes, "Women with warm smiles made much more favorable impressions upon the scientists." This casts Q-sort items like response to humor in a different light. Were the women experiencing positive emotions, or were they performing normative femininity by letting a man think he was funny? The scenario recalls how, in *A Room of One's Own* (1929), Virginia Woolf ruefully remarks that a man's "power to believe in himself" is reliant upon the affirmation of women. "Women have served all these centuries as looking-glasses possessing the magic and delicious power of reflecting the figure of man at twice its natural size." This, Woolf's metaphor suggests, is why men expect women to smile at them, and lash out if they don't.

Indeed, the entire context of the original information gathering was peculiar. Berkeley's IPAR had been founded ten years earlier in 1949 by a psychologist who had spent the war working for the Office of Strategic Services, precursor to the CIA, identifying men who would make good spies. He was renowned for his use of unconventional methods of personality assessment, including administering an early iteration of the Myers-Briggs Personality Inventory. IPAR was established to develop a better understanding of the traits that make successful, creative people tick, and in turn how those traits could be leveraged to bolster the "American way of life" and post-war national security. IPAR's mission was soon folded into serving the imperatives of the emergent Cold War—into identifying the character traits of American exceptionalism in order to defeat the Red Threat. The similarities to Positive Psychology's goals fifty years later are striking.

Striking as well is that IPAR's headquarters had a gendered history not unlike Positive Psychology's founding hot tub party: IPAR's building had previously been a fraternity house, which became a kind of extended joke at the institute. Their unique process of personality assessment involved conducting what were known internally as "house parties," during which groups of ten to twelve subjects would spent three days together under twenty-four-hour scrutiny by staff—almost a kind of hazing. Helson, who would go on to direct the Mills Longitudinal Study, was, for decades, the only woman at these "parties." As Merve Emre notes in *The Personality Brokers* (2018), many of the internal reports prepared by IPAR staff list by name every faculty member, researcher, and grad student involved—all of the men—but often call Helson simply "the woman," despite her professional standing. And it was many of these same men and "the woman" who participated in the day-long, compressed version of the assessment for the participants in the Mills Study, producing the reports that Keltner and Harker used in their own study forty years later.

Keltner and Harker sought to generate contemporaneous observational assessments of the Mills women's photographs. To do so, they hired undergraduates from their intro classes to participate for extra credit. Some of the questions put to these students may as well have asked them to swipe left or right: they were told to draw conclusions about the women's personalities and "interpersonal impact" based solely on what they thought of their photos. This included instructing them to score on a scale from 1 to 5 whether they agreed or disagreed with these four statements: "I would be interested in getting to know her," "I would avoid interacting with her," "I think I would like her," and "I feel I could trust her."

Despite its many obvious design flaws, Keltner and Harker's study is still commonly cited by researchers and taught in classrooms. What is often singled out about the study is the connecting line it draws between happiness and success in heterosexual marriage. Shortly after the publication of Harker and Keltner's findings, the APA featured it as not-to-be-missed research in a piece titled "College Photos Indicate Later Personality Development and Marital Success." In his first popular book for the self-help market, *Authentic Happiness: Using the New Positive Psychology to Realize Your Potential for Lasting Fulfillment* (2002), Seligman describes the study this way: Harker and Keltner "wondered if they could predict from the senior-year smile alone what these women's married lives would turn out to be like. Astonishingly, Duchenne women, on average, were more likely to be married, to stay married, and to experience more personal well-being over the next thirty years." The elision to "Duchenne women" as a type is telling, as is Seligman's narrowing of focus to the women's marriages. Seligman continues to point to the yearbook smiles study as an early success of Positive Psychology, as does Fredrickson, who cited it as recently as this year to support arguments about the relationship impacts of a positive partner.

One of the most disconcerting examples of the study's reach is Marianne LaFrance's use of it in her popular science book *Why Smile? The Science Behind Facial Expressions* (2011). Professor emerita of psychology and women's, gender, and sexuality studies at Yale, LaFrance has been a leading feminist voice in social psychology for decades. Much of her work has focused on the coercive power of patriarchy that makes women's positive emotionality obligatory. Indeed, her criticism of the kind of work they do no doubt explains Keltner and Harker's failure to cite her in their own study. Nonetheless LaFrance's *Why Smile?* appeals to their study as persuasive evidence, suggesting the extent to which its findings have been thoroughly loosed from the specious quality of the research and its misogynist foundations.

AT LEAST the Duchenne smile itself has recently been challenged by researchers at Carnegie Mellon University, who say they have proven that the "smize" indicates nothing more than intensity, including when one is forcing a smile. The Duchenne smile, they argue, can always be—and often is—"fake." It remains to be seen whether the luminaries of Positive Psychology will respond to this challenge to a core doctrine of their field.

For her part, Helson, who died in 2020, was acutely aware of the gendered limitations of her Mills Longitudinal Study. She described her own experience at IPAR and Berkeley as one of daily confrontation with systemic patriarchy and its attendant frustrations, humiliations, and career roadblocks. By the 1980s, she availed herself of the fact that the longitudinal nature of her study permitted a course correction. When she reached out to the Mills research subjects in 1980 to collect the third round of assessments, Helson solicited more nuanced qualitative data, providing opportunities for subjects to address the dramatic society-level changes that had taken place within their lifetimes. She noted that in 1959 the study's subjects had "internalized the narrow margins of a woman's acceptable life—to be married to a promising young man, start a family, and find fulfillment in the homemaker role," adding that, as college students, "ALL of the Mills women wrote that they expected to marry, and nearly all expected children. Those seeking careers were in the minority, and felt their marginality." Thereafter, Helson's research publications began to address these issues and the impacts of the radical movements of the late 1960s and '70s on the Mills women in midlife and later.

In this way, Helson can perhaps best be contextualized as a colleague of Betty Friedan's. The landmark works of both women share a similar methodology. Friedan's 1963 *The Feminine Mystique*, credited with jumpstarting the "second wave" of American feminism, was based on data not dissimilar from that collected by Helson: Friedan had spent the late 1950s gathering information about the marriages, families, work, and social lives of the 1942 graduates of another women's college, Smith, a class to which Friedan herself belonged. Compared to the early decades of the Mills study, Friedan, of course, draws a very different set of conclusions about women's happiness, life outcomes, and well-being. Friedan's "happy housewife heroines" were isolated in lives of quiet, suburban misery, trapped in a gender role that stifled them, overeducated, bored, unfulfilled, and certain there must be something wrong with them because being wives and mothers wasn't enough.

This comparison to Friedan's second-wave feminism throws light on the not-so-carefully disguised conservative qualities of Positive Psychology, as does its resonance with the work of conservative women in the 1970s emergent New Right. These are the women who in large part set the parameters of the ongoing culture wars, and who proved their political potency with the defeat of the Equal Rights Amendment in 1982. They were led by Phyllis Schlafly, a savvy, hard-right Republican political operative who stretched the confines of traditional womanhood while mobilizing them as the root of her power and authority. To counter liberal feminists like Friedan and women's liberationists like Firestone, she appealed to *The Power of the Positive Woman* (1977). In the book, she describes women's and men's roles as naturally distinct and grounded in biology. Against feminists, she argues—as Positive Psychology would later—that women's discontent is all about their own mindsets, not systems:

> The Positive Woman in America today has a near infinite ability to control her own destiny, to reach new heights of achievement, and to motivate and influence others. Her potential is limited only by the artificial barriers erected by a negative view of herself or by the stultifying myths of the women's liberation movement.

Schlafly offers marital advice that in decades to come will be echoed by Seligman, Fredrickson, and Keltner. "With the high divorce rates today, is a happy, lifetime marriage a realistically attainable goal?" queries Schlafly rhetorically. "Of course it is—if you have a positive mental attitude." This extends to her two pillars of a long, happy marriage: the second "is cheerfulness. No other quality can do so much to ensure a happy marriage as a happy disposition." And the first? "A wife must appreciate and admire her husband," in a way that he can see and feel. Surely this includes responding favorably to his humor.

Schlafly didn't invent the caricature of the angry feminist—ugly, unable to get a man, and deeply unhappy, leading her to lash out at normal, joyful women—but she gave it steroids. In her own work, feminist scholar Sara Ahmed recuperates this figure as the "feminist killjoy," a righteously pissed-off, critical woman who refuses patriarchy's inducements to cheerfulness and congeniality. For Ahmed, she is a courageous freedom fighter willing to pay the not-insignificant price for refusing to shut up and just smile. I can't stop thinking about the three Mills women in Harker and Keltner's study who had failed to smile at all for their yearbook pictures. I hope they were the cranky feminist killjoys of Mills College who *refused* to smile when they were told to.

HOW CAPITALISM IS RUINING SEX

Breanne Fahs

SEXUAL PLEASURE is a surprisingly difficult thing to locate and understand. If someone likes something or derives pleasure from it, does that mean that it should no longer be subject to interrogation or critical attention? What does *liking* even mean? Getting off on it? Deriving emotional satisfaction from it? Investing in it as the basis for a relationship that brings joy and satisfaction?

Attempts to ask, and answer, these questions rarely take into account the fact that capitalism has fundamentally altered how people relate to each other, especially in their leisure time. Particularly in the United States, where I study sexuality and have a clinical practice, it is clear that our version of late-stage capitalism—shaped by rampant consumerism, each-for-him/herself neoliberalism, and a lingering anti-sex Puritanism—has limited and twisted our capacity for pleasure. It has done so in particular by stripping away any possibility that does not adhere with the mandates of labor. This focus on work is accompanied by the principle that power and class inequalities are inevitable. And if people must always work, always produce, always operate within and through the logics of capitalism, what happens to sex and sexuality? The answer varies, but in short: nothing good. This is especially acute for women, who suffer worse from the combined effects of capitalism and patriarchy, and whose sexuality and bodily autonomy have historically been treated with disdain.

Modern U.S. life includes a number of features that lessen people's capacity for social relationships, including mind-numbing jobs, uneven shift work, punishingly long work hours, crazed connections to smartphones, soul-crushing commutes, low pay, and destructive coworker and customer interactions. The COVID-19 pandemic has made these facets of people's work lives seem all the more intolerable; the misery of the status quo has driven the Great Resignation and now many workers' refusal to return to the office.

Still, however much workers may start to unravel the rather bleak conditions of their "work–life balance," they nevertheless have become habituated to treat their social connections and intimate relationships more as commodities than as relations with intrinsic value. Capitalism intrudes upon, and infiltrates, seemingly noneconomic aspects of life, such as friendship, leisure, and family life. This impulse is exemplified by a *New York Times* advice column which recommended that people should maintain a wide network of "low stakes, casual friendships." While the author says that such a network has been shown to bring happiness, all of the examples of how it does this are instrumentalist, such as maximizing job prospects.

U.S. capitalism also fundamentally alters the way people have sex—not just the who, what, why, and where, but down to the level of affect: joy, satisfaction, complaint, trauma, anxiety, and unease. In what follows, I outline nine ways that our particular brand of capitalism is destroying people's sex lives, drawing on my experiences as a psychotherapist specializing in sexuality and as a women's studies scholar.

I. Aversion to Leisure and Rest

AT THE FOREFRONT of the capitalist assault on people's sex lives is the fundamental aversion Americans have to leisure, and the sense of suspicion and distrust we have toward those who declare they will rest, play, or goof off. We have the least amount of paid vacation of workers in the Global North, and many U.S. jobs offer no paid time off. The rise of the gig economy has further limited the options that many workers have when they need rest or sick time. And, of course, even Americans who do have paid vacation time often do not take it. We are among the least likely to use our paid vacation, with almost *half* of U.S. paid vacation being forfeited. A study from 2013 found that people have become so accustomed to working and engaging in structured activities that they imagine leisure time as itself a source of intense stress.

We also try to squeeze more productivity out of the day than there are hours. We are among the least well-rested people in the developed world, averaging 6.8 hours of sleep per night, leaving 40 percent of Americans chronically sleep deprived. At least 30 percent of Americans sleep fewer than six hours each night, particularly manufacturing workers and those who work night shifts, such as transportation and health care workers. Sleep-deprived people have lives that start to fall apart: more accidents, conflict with families, declining work and academic performance, more cognitive and health problems, and less attention to sensuality, eating well, and relationships. We are becoming a nation of people whose employers believe that using the restroom is "wasted time."

This normalization of round-the-clock, year-round work—where people prove their dedication to their jobs by overworking and not taking paid leaves, even when they have earned them—introduces a cultural framework where leisure is met with suspicion, contempt, and hostility. Women bear the brunt of this, expected to approach both their work and home lives as jobs, and as a result often end up working nonstop, all day long, in order to meet the demands of their employers and family.

This restlessness is often manifested as a "virtuous" suspicion toward pleasure and rest, meant to distinguish us from pleasure-loving Western Europe (e.g., Italy, Spain, Greece, France) and countries that build naps and rest into the day (e.g., the Philippines, Mexico, Costa Rica, Ecuador, Nigeria). This internalized distrust of pleasure has led to a variety of sexual symptoms that reveal the deep deprior-itization of pleasure and the devaluing of slow-moving sex based on mutuality: we have less time for sex in general, so instead we have "quickies" or fast sex that is typically less pleasurable for women, and virtual sex instead of in-person sex. High percentages of Americans report using their phones while on the toilet (75 percent), in the shower (12 percent), at a place of worship (19 percent), and *during* sex (9–20 percent).

Fahs

II. Orgasm as Producing a Product

PERHAPS THE MOST significant symbol of how the logic of U.S. capitalism intrudes upon and destroys our sex lives is the emphasis on orgasm as a *product*. Here, even the most pleasurable aspects of sex have become surprisingly laborious and tedious, more reminiscent of work than leisure. Sex has begun to mimic a corporate mentality that emphasizes the efficient control of workers' behaviors in order to optimize productivity and minimize the time it takes to complete tasks.

Consider the astonishingly high rates of women faking orgasms (or, producing the "product" expected from sex): my previous work suggests that at least half of women have faked an orgasm, with a significant percentage saying that they have faked often. When my research team asked why they faked orgasms, women described a plethora of reasons: fearing that their (male) partners would be hurt if they did not orgasm, fatigue, wanting the encounter to end, worries about feeling "normal," fears and insecurity about sex in general, and wanting to increase their own arousal. The push to *produce something* has created an environment where women's emotional labor during sex is expected in order to support their partners' egos. Even women who *did* actually orgasm still reported surprisingly low rates of sexual satisfaction, often describing orgasm as "coercive," suggesting that the quest to orgasm can be so cumbersome as to destroy the inherent pleasures of sex itself.

Couples in therapy not infrequently characterize orgasm as necessary for sex to even "count" as sex. "What's the point otherwise?" is a claim I often hear. Sex without orgasm, or sex that does not purposefully drive toward orgasm as a goal, is less and less validated as good sex. In one of my recent studies, several women described feeling pressured to orgasm in order to validate the "work" and "labor" that their partners put into them, as if sex without this form of validation would be meaningless. Orgasm has become an expected product and outcome of sex rather than sex serving as a form of pleasure, connection, fun, or release.

III. Talking About Sex Rather than Having Sex

OUR SUSPICION TOWARD PLEASURE leads sex to become increasingly deprioritized. But because it cannot be fully displaced, it has been supplanted by talking about sex. As cultural theorist Michel Foucault writes, "We have at least invented a different kind of pleasure: . . . the specific pleasure of the true discourse on pleasure." In other words, we enjoy talking about and thinking about sex more than actually having sex. The discourse proliferates, but sex itself does not.

There is an abundance of sexual imagery that pervades U.S. culture, including what sociologist Bernadette Barton has called the "pornification" of everyday life, which includes the rampant use of degrading and raunchy images of women in everything from ads to politics. Sexual content pervades all forms of media we engage with, yet people report a dwindling interest in having sex with partners. At the high end, Americans have sex 6–8 times per month. These numbers seem poised to decline as smartphone use and work hyperconnectivity increase.

In short, people value discourse about sex more than sex itself, which then allows sex to become a product sold, talked about, and imagined in the public marketplace. People make less and less room for sex in their lives, have less and less time to devote to it, and have less and less acknowledgment of its value to their lives in general.

IV. Insistence That Sex Is Dirty

AMERICANS OVERWHELMINGLY FUSE sex and "dirtiness," as U.S. culture has insisted on this as the operating framework for its sexual politics. Indeed, many of our cultural institutions assume, and constantly reinforce, that sex is "filthy"—that this is its baseline truth. Many Americans hear sex discussed as "sin" weekly in their churches (particularly the trope of men being tempted by salacious women). Americans are more religious that anyone else in the Global North, and our churches expend immense energy to contain and control sexuality and to disparage queer sexualities, particularly for teenagers. Some churches sponsor chastity or purity balls, where girls and their fathers attend a wedding-like event, and the girl receives a ring from her father in exchange for a pledge of chastity until marriage. Schools, when they teach sex education at all, insist on teaching sex as risky, disease-ridden, and frightening, prone to violence, the spread of contagions, and devoid of pleasure. Or, more recently, as seen with "Don't Say Gay" laws, there is a collapsing of sex and sexuality such that any discussion of sexual identity is considered tantamount to giving children pornography or attempting to seduce them.

Dirtiness also informs how people formulate sexual fantasies, both during partnered sex and during masturbation. Women learn to fantasize about and eroticize their own lack of agency and power (e.g., being done to rather than doing things to others). Porn is rife with depictions of women that show them as objects of humiliation, degradation, and violence. Talking dirty—an expression that itself links sexuality and "dirtiness"—has also become an increasingly popular way to express sexual desire. Even studying these phenomena as a sex researcher carries the stigma of doing "dirty" work.

These examples collectively suggest that our ability to imagine sexuality outside of dirtiness and taboo has become severely limited. Black poet and critic Audre Lorde offered a distinction between the erotic and the pornographic. The erotic, she held, encompassed the life-sustaining and joy-producing qualities of sex, while the pornographic was power-based, emphasized inequality, and treated sex as dirty. Within this model, it seems clear that our cultural approach to sex lands solidly on the side of the pornographic. We are a culture of Internet sex and quick masturbation rather than one of powerful and slow sexual creativity.

This serves the interests of capitalism. If sex is dirty, people can only experience it as marked with disgust, shame, and taboo, and so sexuality gets cut off from other aspects of their lives—and can be sold back to them at a steep premium. Sex becomes a form of medication for some, obligation for others, mediated phenomenon for still others. People who expect little more from sex than that it be a brief relief will also tolerate pleasureless work lives and joyless office spaces. The more that people rely on mediated versions of their sexuality—through pornographic fantasies, or through powerful institutions that reinforce sex as dirty and bad—the more that sex becomes a force of regression and oppression rather than one of fulfillment, resistance, imagination, or possibility.

V. Dominance/Submission Dynamics

CAPITALISM INSISTS that power imbalances must infuse erotic thought and experience, as much as they do every other aspect of life under itself. People have become so accustomed to power structures, hierarchies, and inequalities in their work lives that they now eagerly recreate those dynamics in their sexual lives as well. The permeation of dominance/submission dynamics—or the insistence that one person is in charge, and the other is not—perpetuates the idea that people cannot share power equally. Sex as a surrendering of power, or a taking of power, has become normative.

As a sex researcher and critical feminist scholar, I don't raise this point to shame anyone about their particular desires, but rather to insist that there is no route to better sex as a culture that does not run through questions of *why* dominance and submission feel desirable to so many of us. I contend that sexual dominance/submission dynamics appeal in part because they reflect back to people what they experience in their everyday lives: a loss of equality, an insistence on submitting to increasingly poor (and underpaid) working conditions, an overvaluation of authority and the power elite, and humiliation as a condition of everyday lives.

U.S. capitalism offers working conditions that fundamentally strip the humanity away from people: they perform emotional labor, they do work without feeling invested in it, they feel tired and stressed out, they dislike coworkers and bosses (and rarely feel solidarity with coworkers against their bosses), they endure long commutes and difficult working conditions, and they have little creativity, autonomy, or control over their work lives. Capitalism normalizes dominance and submission, control of labor and time, and fundamental inequalities among and between people/workers. U.S. capitalism, in particular, requires working constantly to the point of exhaustion. This framework goes against mutuality, shared decision-making, connectivity, and pleasure between partners.

VI. Negativity Toward Emotions and Desires

UNDER CAPITALISM, a good worker is one who has tight control over his or her emotions and does not show big feelings on the job. Efficiency and product-oriented thinking are prioritized, while emotions, affect, intuition, and desires are not. All of this leads to a certain type of alienation in which people engage in meaningless actions and feel estranged from any sense of feelings within themselves.

This equation also transfers into people's sex lives. People avoid their emotions during sex or seek out sex without emotional connections. They look for (or tolerate) "friends with benefits" relationships where sex is "just sex," or want open relationships where they will not have romantic feelings for other partners. Similarly, sex as sport, or the belief that emotions ruin or lessen sexual empowerment, have also shown up in how people think about sexuality.

A recent rise in the popularity of noncommitted relationships and relationships without emotional connections has created a number of problems for people's sexual and emotional lives, particularly as people idealize emotionless sex and devalue emotional vulnerability. Research on friends-with-benefits relationships, for example, shows that they valorize traditionally "masculine" forms of intimacy (no emotions, no strings attached) while devaluing "feminine" approaches that emphasize emotional presence. Women in such relationships often feel more distress, guilt, and shame than do men. Though many people assume the opposite is true, in practice casual sex rarely offers a successful subversion of cultural norms and instead all too often reinforces traditional gender and sexual scripts.

Our culture does no better when it comes to fantasy and sexual desire in the abstract. Sex education programs do not typically even mention sexual fantasy as part of early sexual life, just as most partners do not regularly discuss sexual fantasies with each other. In therapy, my clients are not typically curious about where their fantasies come from, or what they might mean, instead choosing to analyze the behavioral or negotiating aspects of their sexual lives (e.g., how often they have sex with their partners and whether to initiate or agree to sex). The cerebral or imaginative/creative qualities of their sex lives are, more often than not, left out in the cold. This is yet another way that U.S. capitalism has influenced thinking about sexuality, reducing sex to mechanical bodies producing a product (orgasm) rather than envisioning sexuality as a part of creativity and humanness.

VII. Fusion of Sex and Consumerism

CAPITALISM TEACHES PEOPLE that consumption is a necessary part of their everyday lives, and that they should direct all aspects of their lives toward the accumulation of more things. This infects people's sex lives in numerous ways.

First, people allow pornography—a genre that largely lacks sexual creativity, especially mainstream pornography—to train and reinforce certain kinds of sexual fantasies and desires at the expense of all others. Common themes in pornography include women "servicing" men, violence against women, forced or coerced sex, stark power imbalances, role playing with women dressed as young girls, and racist imagery.

Second, people often turn to sex toys to help them fulfill or enhance their sex lives. This means that women increasingly masturbate using sex toys instead of their fingers, and partnered sex more often includes devices and gadgets meant to enhance sexual pleasure. Sex toys can change people's sense of their sexual possibilities. In one of my recent studies on women's masturbation, several women mentioned that they did not know how to masturbate without a sex toy, and that masturbating without a toy was unthinkable. Sex toys must be purchased —and many are quite expensive—which turns sexual pleasure into something that can only be achieved via commercial products. And, while feminist sex toy shops have grown in number and visibility, most sex toy shops do not openly embrace feminist politics.

Third, our leisure time—potentially time to rest, have sex, unwind, or socialize—has become increasingly shaped and molded by consumerism, in that people associate relaxation with consumption

Fahs

(e.g., shopping, traveling, beauty treatments). If relaxation becomes equated with buying things or consuming, our leisure time is then susceptible to corporate intrusions, the pressures of advertising, social comparisons with others, and the hazards of overspending. By contrast, people direct little time and attention toward the pleasures of rest, social interaction outside of consuming, face-to-face interactions, spending time in nature, or simply wasting time.

VIII. Sex Work Without Sex Workers

UNDER CAPITALISM, imagining sex as work rather than play has permeated people's sexual lives—and we all know that work is meant to be serious. Even actors in pornography rarely laugh, goof around, or seem to have any fun, despite the fact that porn began as a genre of humor. The link between sex and work appears in the cultural lexicon surrounding sex, thus providing a window into how language reflects the priorities and logic of capitalism. The terms "blow job" and "hand job" both imply that women who give men oral and manual sex are *working*. Traces of sex work and sexual labor show up in even the most mundane descriptions of sexuality, particularly the ways that women describe different kinds of sexual performances (e.g., moaning, showing enjoyment, mitigating damage to a partner's ego) or different ways of displaying "authentic" sexual feelings.

Moreover, many feminists have started to think of "sex work" as including not just paid sexual labor but also the unpaid sexual labor that occurs in the mundane sexual relationships women have with men. What would it mean to acknowledge that nearly all sexually active women are engaging in "sex work"? If we broaden the conceptualization of "sex workers" to include those who associate sex with work—that is, those who labor to create sexual experiences for their partner, or those who think of sex as yet another chore—the notion of who engages in sexual labor expands considerably. Traces of sex work appear everywhere in women's descriptions of their sexual lives, from explicit sexual exchanges (e.g., women giving husbands oral sex in exchange for them doing the dishes) to implicit notions of validating sexual labor (e.g., loudly moaning during sex to show that a partner's sexual efforts had positive outcomes).

Conceptualizing all of this as "sex work" shines a light on how commonplace such labor is, and contextualizes more overt forms of sex work (e.g., for-pay sex work) as simply one small subset of a larger cultural pattern.

IX. Foreclosure of Sexual Possibilities

PERHAPS THE SINGLE MOST catastrophic way that U.S. capitalism destroys our sex lives is by foreclosing certain kinds of sexual possibilities. As feminist philosopher Avital Ronell writes in *Stupidity* (2002): "Work makes people stupid, depriving them of essential types of nonproduction, leisure, meditation, play. It becomes ethically necessary to find a way rigorously to affirm nonworking, to subsidize rest, laziness, lolling around without succumbing to common criminalizations or devaluations of the logic of other 'activities.'" Similar to the ways that capitalism makes it difficult to imagine other kinds of economic and social structures, sex in this culture lacks imagination. It becomes static, predictable, driven underground, quarantined to the bedroom, and cordoned off from other aspects of our lives. People stop asking what else sex could be, what else it could look like. They stop imagining differently.

The foreclosure of sexual possibilities—a process heightened by people's traumatic experiences of the pandemic and the deep misogyny embedded in the recent loss of abortion rights—means that sex rarely works as a creative force but mostly serves as a regressive one. People cannot demand more of their sexual culture—movies, pornography, books, sex education curricula, schooling, partnerships, and more—because they, too, cannot imagine differently. We must make room for a sexuality full of rebellious impulses, creativity, inspiration, fervor, energy, and power, one that stands in opposition to capitalism. How could sex serve as a force that undermines or even destroys the oppressive institutions of our time?

People may never cultivate a sexuality entirely free—of cultural constraints, problematic and oppressive practices and structures, and inequalities—but we are already *freer than we feel*. If the COVID-19 pandemic has taught us anything, it is that the rules are flimsy and easily breakable, that entire systems and structures can be toppled and rearranged, that people's relationship to work and leisure can and must change. The fall of *Roe v. Wade*, too, has shown that rights are never inevitable, progress is a painfully jagged story, and that sex itself is always being shaped and molded by the forces of the day.

Could we imagine a sexuality that takes its time, loves leisure and fun and play, has no product or goal in mind, sees something else possible in partners and ourselves? Is there room for a sexuality that imagines that it is freer than it feels, that continually conjures something different? Can new forms of sexuality draw from new frameworks of justice and resistance? Can we make a defiant pleasure politics of bodies and sexualities that springs up from, rather than exists in denial of, the bleak political landscape of anti-abortion legislation, transphobic policies, anti-fat bullying, and anti-Black police violence? Can we ask of sex that it transforms the world rather than replicates the worst aspects of it? There is an urgency to this: to not allow U.S.-style capitalism to hollow out these sexual possibilities, to insist on something more.

PLEASURE ACTIVISM

adrienne maree brown

PLEASURE ACTIVISM is the work we do to reclaim our whole, satisfiable selves from the impacts of oppression and supremacy. Pleasure activism asserts that we all need and deserve pleasure, and that our social structures must reflect this. In this moment, we must prioritize the pleasure of those most impacted by oppression.

Pleasure activists seek to understand and learn from the politics and power dynamics of everything that makes us feel good. This includes sex and the erotic, drugs, fashion, humor, passion work, connection, reading, cooking and eating, music and other arts, and so much more. Pleasure activism acts from an analysis that pleasure is a natural, safe, and liberated part of life—and that we can offer each other tools and education to make sure sex, desire, drugs, connection, and other pleasures aren't life-threatening or harming but rather life-enriching.

Pleasure activists believe that, by tapping into the potential goodness in each of us, we can generate justice and liberation, growing a healing abundance where we have been socialized to believe only scarcity exists. Ultimately, pleasure activism is us learning to make justice and liberation the most pleasurable experiences we can have on this planet.

Pleasure activism is not about generating or indulging in excess. Sometimes when I bring up this work to people, I can see a bacchanalia unfold behind their eyes, and it makes me feel tender. I think because most of us are so repressed, our fantasies go to extremes to counterbalance all that contained longing. Pleasure activism is about learning what it means to be satisfiable, to generate, from within and from between us, an abundance from which we can all have enough.

Part of the reason so few of us have a healthy relationship with pleasure is because a small minority of our species hoards the excess of resources, creating a false scarcity and then trying to sell us back our own joy. Some think it belongs to them, that it is their inheritance. Some think it a sign of their worth, their superiority. White people and men have been the primary recipients of this delusion, the belief that they deserve to have excess while the majority doesn't have enough—and, further, that the majority exists to please them.

A central aspect of pleasure activism is tapping into the natural abundance that exists within and between us, and between our species and this planet. Pleasure is not one of the spoils of capitalism. It is what our bodies, our human systems, are structured for; it is the aliveness and awakening, the gratitude and humility, the joy and celebration of being miraculous.

So rather than encouraging moderation over and over, I want to ask you to relinquish your own longing for excess and to stay mindful of your relationship to enough. How much sex would be enough? How high would be high enough? How much love would feel like enough? Can you imagine being healed enough? Happy enough? Connected enough? Having enough space in your life to actually live it? Can you imagine being free enough?

Do you understand that you, as you are, are enough?

HOW MANY OF US are trapped in a politically regressive loop of desire?

How many of us—even as we hone a feminist or womanist or post-gender or otherwise radical politics around who we are, relative to power—regress in bed into submission practices we are taught are biological, primal, even spiritual? I suspect many of the most powerful women are still convinced that in bed we need to be dragged by our hair into a cave and ravaged by a lover who plays a traditionally patriarchal role of dominance.

A key aspect of smashing the patriarchy will be examining not just rape culture but our culture of desire. Not with shame or with righteousness but with deep curiosity: What are your go-to fantasies? What turns you on, and can you change it if it doesn't align with what you believe?

Through attraction we feel for others, media images, and healthy and unhealthy interactions with those older than us, visuals and stories groove a pathway for desire in our brains. We begin to have certain scenarios that turn us on, fantasies of what we want to do or have done to us or witness. Fantasy is often a safe space to desire things that we might never do or allow in real life.

For most of us, this desire-setting happens early, and if we aren't both careful and creative, we can get stuck in fantasies that don't mature and politicize with us. We can get caught in fantasies that perpetuate things so counter to our beliefs and values that we feel ashamed of what we want, even as we find ways to get it.

I had a babysitter when I was quite young who liked to watch *Porky's* (1981), which I can best describe as a rape culture time capsule from the eighties. My family's military-issue apartment was small, and I easily snuck out of bed and found a spot from which I took in sexually disempowering images I didn't understand. I also loved musicals—*Grease* (1978) and *Seven Brides for Seven Brothers* (1954) were favorites. As a result of this kind of media, my early fantasy life was often about men taking advantage of skinny women, secretly watching them, trapping them, or women having to change for the desires of men. I thought this was how sex happens, that it centers men, and that we as women should be in a constant state of seducing, playing hard to get, and getting caught by men.

Hence, my twenties. But I learned! To see differently, to imagine differently.

I once got to swim in a body of water where saltwater met freshwater. With goggles on, I could see the subtle horizontal line between the freshwater on top and the heavier, denser seawater below. That visual comes to mind as I think of the cultures in which we swim in the United States. The heavier seawater is our much-defended rape culture, which is fed by fantasies of incest, rape, coercion, boundary transgression, force, transaction, and scenarios where the masculine wields power over the feminine. Floating above that is the culture of repression, often rooted in religious spaces. Repression fantasies focus on purity, innocence, virginity, monogamy, and youth.

These fantasies train us in the gender-normative behaviors that sustain our layered culture. We learn from parents, teachers, extended family, media, religious leaders, and basically all adults we encounter. And, of course, our early lovers, who are often fumbling in their own confusion and learning.

Men learn to be dominant, initiating penetrators: they learn that it's in their nature to ravish women. Women learn to be coy, dishonest receptacles: we're taught to say no until the last moment—and then say nothing but yes. Or say nothing and mean yes. Those who don't fit into this binary construction, or who shift within it in their lifetimes, are often expected to still don these roles in sexual encounters. The lessons are sometimes very direct, other times implied: cross your legs like a lady, save that for your husband, take her like a man, it hurts a little at first, it's just nature, who's your Daddy.

Layer into this our intersecting systems of hierarchy—racism, ableism, classism, etc.—and you have a plethora of fantasies that perpetuate and sustain a janky reality. These gendered fantasies shape our very sense of self. How do I fit in this world? Am I desirable? How do I become desirable? What role must I play? Do I take or give?

So few people make it to this question: What do I really want?

From our first moments, we should be encouraged to focus on how our bodies feel, what sensations and interactions awaken us, what feels wrong, what kind of touch feels right, and how to communicate a spectrum of boundaries and consent. Instead, many of us spend our formative years in our heads, learning to be something we are not, unlearning the skills of truth we're all born with. Eventually our desires are woven so thoroughly with these social norm fantasies that we think that we desire our own disempowerment or someone else's.

I have been intentionally working on developing new fantasies. Fantasy is where I first explored the impossible idea that I am desirable. The improbable idea that fat bodies, brown and Black bodies, scarred and dimpled bodies, bodies that hurt and lurch and roll, bodies with hair and acne, bodies that sweat and make sounds and messes—that *all* of our bodies—are desirable. This work has shifted my reality of lovers and my reality of how I see myself and let myself be treated.

And, and, and . . . even as I write this, I won't tell you all of my fantasies. Some of them are rooted so deeply in my system that I'm not sure I'll ever let them go—I'm not even sure I want to. But I do want to be able to recognize what is mine and what isn't, what should stay in fantasy and what is aligned with the world I'm generating—one in which gender is not an indication of power in or out of the bedroom.

ON THIS JOURNEY of liberating our desire, we have to look at our relationship to pornography. We should use a harm reduction approach, to learn to look at our practices without judgment, without shaming, but with curiosity and agency. What shapes us as we turn to pornography? How does porn, in turn, shape our real-life desires? And can we use pornography to shape our real-world desires?

I am particularly interested in what our pornographic practices do to our imaginations.

Back in the day, meaning before I was born, pornography was mostly in the form of still images. You looked at a Polaroid of people having sex, a black-and-white still of a woman splayed on a chaise lounge, or a *Kama Sutra* drawing, and your mind did the rest of the work. Your imagination animated the scene, imagining your fingers moving across the flesh that you never actually saw in motion, building erotic charge. Now, everything is POV, high-definition porn or amateur porn shot on peoples' phones. You can watch badly acted porn or skip to pounding porn without any storyline. You can tune into live people who will respond to your text requests to touch themselves while you watch. The instant your mind begins to move in any direction of desire, you can type your longing into a search bar and watch your fantasy or something close to it.

Your imagination isn't really needed.

And perhaps that would be fine if the top searches were "woman on top of someone she could never identify as a family member," "strapped women taking tender tushes," "grown-up legal-aged professionals of all genders in hot consensual anti-racist role play." But we know that they aren't. In 2016 the top pornography searches for men included "stepmom," "stepsister," "mom," "teen," and "stepmom and son." Men also liked videos in the categories of "Japanese," "Ebony," and "Asian," in that order. Women were searching for "stepdad and daughter," as well as "gangbang" and "extreme gangbang." They wanted to see "big Black dick," or just "Black sex" in general, and sometimes "Japanese." (That appears to heavily overlap with specific kinks like foot worship, breast worship, and sexual games.) And everyone wanted to see "lesbians." These aren't the only things people were searching for, but they were the top searches for millions of people the world over according to Pornhub, which at that time was the most visited porn site in the world.

How do we face the truth that our trending fantasies center around incest, underage lovers, racialized power dynamics, and sexual encounters in which women are objects? How do we face ourselves and what we've been programmed to desire, especially if it works against our sense of agency and connection and integrity in our real-life sex? How do we move *beyond* the things we have accidentally come to want and *toward* our desires to break the intersecting cycles of harm we are in? And how do we face the deeply embedded shame around what we desire? Because while we didn't create the water we're swimming in, it's still poisoning us.

How do we take responsibility for the ways in which we are programming ourselves to participate in rape culture in the deepest recesses of our minds? And that our imaginations are being discarded in the process? What is the consequence of discarded erotic imagination?

I believe our imaginations—particularly the parts of our imaginations that hold what we most desire, what brings us pleasure, what makes us scream yes—are where we must seed the future, turn toward justice and liberation, and reprogram ourselves to desire sexually and erotically empowered lives.

Ideally, porn is a spark for, and an extension of, a vibrant sexual imagination. And just like with fantasy, we may choose to continue watching stuff beyond our politics, stuff we never plan to practice—but this should be an intentional, informed sexual choice.

This begins by examining our search bars, finding our collective dignity. It could also include writing ourselves into original erotica and porn scripts or trying out some new pornographic narratives that are fully feminist, so that we can experience sexy content without some built-in cost of collaborating in our own oppression.

I HAVE BEGUN TO SEE pleasure activism all around me. Pleasure reminds us to enjoy being alive. Our misery only serves those who wish to control us, to have our existence be in service to their own. True pleasure—joy, happiness, and satisfaction—has been the force that helps us move beyond the constant struggle, that helps us live and generate futures beyond this dystopian present, futures worthy of our miraculous lives.

Pleasure—embodied, connected pleasure—is one of the ways we know when we are free. That we are always free. That we always have the power to cocreate the world. Pleasure helps us move through the times that are unfair, through grief and loneliness, through the terror of genocide, or days when the demands are just overwhelming. Pleasure heals the places where our hearts and spirits get wounded. Pleasure reminds us that, even in the dark, we are alive. Pleasure is a medicine for the suffering that is absolutely promised in life.

Pleasure is the point. Feeling good is not frivolous, it is freedom.

THE DEMOCRATIC POTENTIAL OF CRUISING
Jack Parlett

"ANOTHER HUNDRED PEOPLE just got off of the train," sings one of the characters in Stephen Sondheim's 1970 musical *Company*. This lyrical refrain captures not only the daily mass of people who flood into New York City, but the sheer amount of romantic possibility offered by this numbers game. The song, titled "Another Hundred People," gestures toward the dating lives of the play's central characters, and to the possibilities of finding intimacy in a "city of strangers." But for clued-in listeners, the song's focus on the anonymous crowd also contains a hidden message. The song's mention of city dwellers who "find each other" in the "crowded streets and the guarded parks," by the "rusty fountains" and the "dusty trees with the battered barks," may not seem unusual at first blush—but these lyrics, written by a gay New Yorker for a musical nominally about heterosexual characters, are also clearly about cruising, the practice of searching for sexual connection among strangers in public places, notably streets, parks, and public bathrooms.

Cruising is often, though not exclusively, urban and gay. The term has existed since at least the early 1900s, when "cruiser" was used concurrently with "streetwalker" to describe the men selling sex on New York's Bowery. The term's nautical resonance aptly describes cruising's particular temporality. Just as one is said to take a cruise in, rather than to, a location, the cruiser's search for sex is less a predetermined journey from A to B than it is an act of floating within an experience.

Cruising, as an impromptu way of connecting with strangers, exemplifies what is best about both cities and queer life. In *Sex in Public* (1998), queer scholars Lauren Berlant and Michael Warner talk about this in terms of queer culture's "mobile sites," transient "counter-intimacies" composed of "lyric moments that interrupt the hostile cultural narrative." As a form of spontaneous human connection, cruising borrows from and extends the potential of the city as a democratizing space, one that brings us into everyday contact with people we do not know, with people who seem unlike us until we realize our shared desires.

THE RECENT MONKEYPOX OUTBREAK, and the related public health messaging about safe sexual practices among queer people, is just the latest example of the way cruising culture is contingent upon changing social and environmental conditions. Cruising, like the cities in which it most often occurs, has changed over time; it makes little sense to speak about it in ahistorical terms. And any historical approach to cruising must begin with the fact that its early conflation with streetwalking acknowledged their shared criminality: as the remit of homosexual men, cruising was illegal for much of its history whether money changed hands or not. But as George Chauncey shows in his landmark 1994 history *Gay New York: Gender, Urban Culture, and the Making of the Gay Male World 1890–1940*, cruising, though heavily criminalized, flourished in the city in the early twentieth century. Often lacking private quarters where they could act upon their desires, men of different social classes would frequent an array of public spots where they knew they could meet other men for sex. As a network of signals mostly illegible to straight people, ranging from a simple look to increasingly sophisticated codes—most famously the hanky code—cruising was both an expediency and a lifeline, a way for gay men to find each other. As Frank O'Hara wrote in the poem "Homosexuality" (written in 1954, though unpublished until 1970), "It's wonderful to admire oneself with / complete candor / tallying up the merits of the latrines."

If cruising offered a mode of solidarity and survival in the decades before Stonewall and gay liberation, it then became, in turn, a visible expression of sexual liberation in the 1970s. But its valence soon changed again in the 1980s, when the HIV/AIDS epidemic politicized gay men's negotiation of risk and anonymity when it came to choosing sexual partners. Cruising (and its criminalization, for that matter) hardly disappeared in the era of safe sex, though: the infamous public outing of singer George Michael in the late 1990s followed his arrest for engaging in "lewd acts" with an undercover cop in a park bathroom in Beverly Hills.

Alongside the implications of HIV/AIDS, the advent of online dating technologies would also alter the reliance upon cruising as a mode of connection. From the popular chat rooms of the early 2000s to the launch of the GPS-driven hookup app Grindr in 2009, the technologization of cruising in more recent years has complicated our narratives of its democratic potential. But the idea that cruising might offer an equitable and meaningful mode of togetherness has a long history in American letters, and it is worth revisiting these to reflect on what is at risk of being lost if cruising were to finally disappear as a practice.

Celebrations of the democratic power of cruising can be traced back at least as far as Walt Whitman, an early prophet of urban queer culture. For Whitman, Manhattan, a "city of orgies," provided both an enactment of, and analogy for, a new democratic vision of the United States. This vision of a utopian country centered "adhesiveness" and "comradeship," the "beautiful and sane affection of man for man," powered by the looks between passing strangers and the new kinds of belonging they might presage. The look of cruising, something Whitman in "Song of the Open Road" calls the "talk of those turning eyeballs," brings to light a dream of the good life that is equal parts nostalgic and future-oriented—the sense, as he puts it in "To a Stranger," that "I have somewhere surely lived a life of joy with you," and will yet again. In this way, Whitman suggests that cruising can be central to the nation-building work of constructing "imagined community" of the kind described by Benedict Anderson, that mental formation of others one may never properly meet but who nevertheless constitute a people, albeit a subterranean one in this case.

Although Whitman frequented establishments with homosocial reputations, such as Pfaff's in Greenwich Village, and wrote about the power of an amorous look in a crowded tavern, there is something distinctive in his work about passing glances out in public, among the urban multitude, where you could share a moment of fantasy with any number of people. It is a kind of connection that is able to transgress many of the ordinarily social categories that keep us apart, and is therefore quite distinct even from the kind of cruising that happens within the economic choreography of bars.

An admiration of public cruising of the sort that Whitman's work exhibits was so baked in to queer U.S. identity that even a century later, it remained much the same. In his series of images of Christopher Street in the 1970s, photographer Sunil Gupta pursued an artistic project that would have made Whitman proud, photographing the men who caught his eye on the street in the gay environs of Chelsea. In the sexual boom of the gay liberation years, there were, as Gupta would later remember, so many men and so little time. While a productive night could be had at the bar or the bathhouse, there were still many other people you could be yet to meet and hook up with. Gupta's Christopher Street photographs figure this abundance by embracing the streets as a site of possibility. Together with Whitman's poems of encounter, almost a century earlier, these images offer a way of thinking about cruising as not only, or even primarily, about hooking up, but about the communal power of eroticized looking, flashes of affinity that may not lead directly to sexual consummation, but are an important way of situating yourself within a shared community.

Cruising often created the community that it wished existed. On the western end of Christopher Street squatted the dilapidated Hudson River piers. Post-Stonewall but pre-AIDS, the long-abandoned buildings functioned as cruising sites where men could meet and have sex. Because they were de facto public spaces, they were more racially and economically diverse cruising spaces than gay establishments that cost money (for the cover, to buy drinks) and tended to be aimed at attracting a specific clientele. For example, gay bathhouses, in some ways the most efficient sexual spaces for those looking to hook up, were often deeply hierarchical, however much the shedding of clothes would seem to transgress the categories of value in the everyday outside. Bars, similarly, had an aesthetic focus. The piers, although sometimes dangerous, offered an alternative. In her book *Cruising the Dead River* (2019), about the waterfront and artist David Wojnarowicz, Fiona Anderson notes that many of those who cruised the piers were excluded from the West Village bars, and often "homeless, overweight, disabled, older, poor . . . African American or Latinx."

Further uptown, where Disney mascots now vie for tourist photos and the new production of *Company* is playing, was the pre-Giuliani Times Square, a red-light district of cheap luncheonettes and pornographic movie theaters. The relative anonymity among the low lights of the cinema provided another space for interracial and interclass cruising, as famously eulogized by Samuel R. Delany in *Times Square Red, Times Square Blue* (1999). Delany, who frequented the theaters and often met sexual partners there, recalls that the cinemas were places that New Yorkers socialized with people of truly different backgrounds. In the book's conclusion, Delany describes this sort of "contact" across socioeconomic boundaries as the "lymphatic system of a democratic metropolis," whether it's cruising for sex or "any number of other forms" of social encounter, from "waiting for the public library to open" to "coming down to sit on the stoop on a warm day."

WHILE THE TIMES SQUARE establishments Delany describes had already been erased by gentrification by the time *Times Square Red, Times Square Blue* was published, this blueprint for a "cosmopolitan culture" based around everyday contact, the basis of an erotic commons, has held true. But while there are still numerous places in the city the heritage cruiser can visit, numerous bars or clubs for queer people to "find each other," something of this public sexual culture, a culture of live and contingent encounters, has faded. Public encounters have largely been replaced by more mediated forms of hooking up online or through apps, a move from the street to the screen. In this substitution of the live and sensory experience of physical proximity for its virtualization, through profile photos and measurements of distance in feet via GPS, cruising's relation to personhood has inevitably changed too.

Attempts to reckon meaningfully with the way cruising has been changed by hookup apps like Grindr often begin by conceding that, on the surface, "dating and hookup media are terrible in every way," as Tom Roach writes in his book *Screen Love: Queer Intimacies in the Grindr Era* (2021). The "laundry list of horrors essentially writes itself," he continues.

> These media are steeped in a consumerist logic. They substitute algorithms for pheromones. They instrumentalize intimacy and mechanize the wily ways of desire. . . . They exacerbate the same barbarous impulses—hyper-individualism, cutthroat competition, solipsism, and self-aggrandizement—so integral to and rewarded in the marketplace.

Parlett

While it may not be responsible for creating them in the first place, an app culture structured in this way at least energizes all manner of exclusionary attitudes and practices, including microaggressions and discriminations along axes of race, gender, and body type that are passed off as mere "preferences". In contrast to this reification of public erotic contact, cruising's original copy looks all the more appealing, a contingent, flesh-and-blood alternative to an interface in which encounters can often seem overdetermined before they have even been initiated with a cursory "Hey."

I have certainly found myself pining for cruising's more retro iterations, aware that my research interests in urban sexual cultures are informed by my own desire to feel closer to an erotic life that doesn't center upon the same device I use to check email and call my mom. But discontent with the present can falsify the past, particularly for those, like myself, who weren't firsthand witnesses to the supposed halcyon days. In his book *Pier Groups: Art and Sex Along the New York Waterfront* (2019), an art history of the piers, Jonathan Weinberg notes how "we love to complain that the virtual world of the internet, computers and cell phones has destroys our humanity," meaning that "accounts of sex and romantic relationships today are built around a longing for a past when people supposedly had more authentic connections with one another." But the anonymous sexual cultures of the past, Weinberg suggests, even in the more socially open spaces of the piers, were not some warm or democratic or edifying paradise lost; less an alternative to the "supposed alienation of the early twenty-first century" than an antecedent. For theorists such as Roach, it is precisely digital cruising's estranging qualities that also light upon its potential for rethinking society and selfhood. Because contemporary cruising media are "so thoroughly saturated in neoliberal market relational norms, they offer an opportunity to reconceive liberal-humanist notions of the social altogether." As anthropologist Shaka McGlotten puts it, there is little sense in distinguishing too readily between the virtual and the real, insofar as "intimacy is already virtual in the ways it is made manifest through affective experience." There is no pure cruising space, outside space and time and untouched by metaphors of media or marketplace.

As Roach goes on to show in *Screen Love*, the "laundry list of horrors" may go too far in writing off hookup apps like Grindr and Scruff as irremediably awful. They have, after all, also enabled new social and sexual possibilities for users, particularly in locations outside of urban centers, where cruising has historically been extremely limited and not infrequently dangerous. Even within cities, we mustn't romanticize away the fact that cruising could be extremely dangerous: encounters often went awry and turned into robberies, beatings, and even murders. The anonymity of an app interface's grid, that glut of floating torso pictures and blank profiles, may contribute to a feeling of glassy virtuality, but it also offers users safety and discretion. In *Queer Silence: On Disability and Rhetorical Absence* (2022), gender studies scholar J. Logan Smilges recuperates that bane of apps, the blank profile, which Smilges notes are more common among users for whom it may be less safe to be out. Smilges argues that these blank profiles can be a way for users to reject the pressure to perform a particular kind of identity within the erotic economy of an app—a kind of placeholder visibility for those for whom visibility remains complex.

And while apps like Grindr may have been created for hooking up, they have come to be used for other purposes. As Eli Martin, chief marketing officer for the hookup site Sniffies, puts it: "Grindr's really become like a Facebook. It's like you can go on there and you can find anything. You can find a boyfriend; you can maybe sell a car. Who knows, find your best friend." Within this ecology of hookup apps, Sniffies seeks to fulfill a "superspecific" function of facilitating more-or-less instantaneous hookups. It aims to do this by displaying results on a map of your neighborhood—as opposed to a list—an interface that in effect returns to cruising's old-fashioned topography by showing where users are in real time. A little open-door icon even glosses if a person is capable of hosting sex right where they are, which may be only steps from you.

To observe that "another hundred people" just logged on to the app may not have the same romantic ring as urban narratives of the past have primed us to want. But to dismiss the efficacies of the digital cruising world would be, as Roach notes, to remain ignorant of the fact that "screen-mediated discourse is an integral component of contemporary communication"; we "cannot return to some fictional unmediated past." Perhaps the most crystalline description of the realities of cruising today can be found in a line from poet Danez Smith: "everyone on the app says they hate the app but no one stops." This poem, titled "a note on the phone app that tells me how far I am from other men's mouths," and published in Smith's 2016 collection *Don't Call Us Dead*, reflects on the absurdities and racial politics of this landscape of "headless horsehung horsemen." It in turn captures a collective feeling, the sense that apps are divisive and ambivalent but central to queer sexual culture, a sentiment about cruising that is hardly unique to the contemporary era.

If the goal of cruising is, ultimately, for people to "find each other," for anything from a momentary frisson to a full-blown sexual encounter, the ends of digital versus IRL cruising are altogether similar, even if the means make them feel wildly different. And while cruising can be associated with cold expediency, a way of getting your kicks without the rigmarole of conventional dating, it has often felt to me like a kind of anonymous support network, whether I've accessed it on an app or during a foray to the storied pastures of certain parts of North London. Perhaps this says more about my approach than it does the act itself, but this particular kind of solidarity is an important aspect of cruising's communal potential.

There is certainly no guarantee you'll feel sated or validated or otherwise better after hooking up, but implicit in even the most cursory cruising encounter is, in my experience, the shared admission of a vulnerability, and of loneliness, perhaps, an unspoken basis of the desire to come together. To cruise is, in its most basic sense, to tap into a community whose only logic is desire itself, even if this improvised grouping is far from homogenous, and rarely even harmonious. Like Delany, I have met people cruising whom I'm unlikely to have met otherwise. That these encounters have seldom developed into lasting relationships or friendships, even after improbably revealing moments of pillow talk within the same hour of learning each other's names, is precisely the point. You never know who or what you'll find in a city of strangers. That's part of democracy's promise, too.

LUNCHTIME IN ITALY
Jonathan Levy

THE MORNING AFTER the 2016 U.S. presidential election, my partner Skyped her parents back home in Italy. I finished my coffee, and they chatted. At some point her mother asked where I was: I had broken my usual pattern of dropping in to say *ciao*. My partner slid the laptop over to direct the camera's gaze at my head, slumped onto our dining room table. "What happened?" the voice on the computer asked. "Trump won," I explained.

It is not that my in-laws did not appreciate the gravity of the event; they were stunned too. Born under Mussolini, they preferred to look fondly upon the United States whenever possible. After all, the U.S. Army helped liberate their country from fascism. Like many outside the United States, and unlike many Americans, they appreciate the power the U.S. government enjoys abroad. After sharing in the dour mood, to console me, my mother-in-law asked, "Well . . . what is there for lunch?"

The question was a nudge back from the brink of political despair. But many questions could have accomplished that end. She asked about lunchtime. Having been visiting Italy regularly for over a decade, I could understand why.

Lunchtime in Italy is not only about what to eat for lunch. It is also about time. The event halts the day. In places like Viterbo, the provincial medieval town of 60,000 outside Rome where my in-laws live, the city nearly completely shuts down. One has little choice but to engage in the ritual. A tablecloth must be spread, a table fully set. Timeworn recipes; the food, even if abundant, should be basic and familiar, not indulgent or creative. Surely, a glass of wine. The sociality of the event is important. Lunchtime must be marked with others, the meal lingered over communally. Whenever American friends or family visit us here, at some point they usually give me the look: "When will this *ever* end?" It ends when the espresso arrives to even out the wine and to properly launch reentry back into the working day.

True—for many Italians, lunchtime is more a widely shared aspiration than a daily reality. The steady rise of dual-income households has threatened the practice, which long found women in the kitchen, preparing the meal. In cities much larger than Viterbo, the workday does not allow for lunchtime. Even in Viterbo, in recent years outside the medieval wall a rim of big box retail stores popped up that do not close for lunch. Workers take a U.S.-style lunchbreak; they do not enjoy an Italian-style lunchtime. Still, even if not everybody can participate in it every day, the ideal of lunchtime lives on in Italy. It survived the whistles and bells of industrial clock time, the mechanized factory stroke. Very likely, it will survive the threats of today.

My mother-in-law's question left an impression on me then, which has only continued to resonate since. We left the United States in the summer of 2020, and our family has spent most of the pandemic in Italy, much of it in Viterbo. Living here, I have become passionately invested in lunchtime. I could go on at length about how good the food is. But no less, I have found the unhurried daily rituals of the communal event—especially the demand that the day if at all possible should be organized around it—soothing and anchoring.

Is there anything worth making of this feeling? I have come to believe my *suocera*'s question reveals something important that has gone very wrong with U.S. life. From abroad these past two years, at times homesick, as I watched the United States experience COVID-19, the election of 2020, January 6, QAnon, the early years of the Biden presidency, thousands of mass shootings, the reversal of *Roe v. Wade*, talk of a "crisis of democracy" in the United Sates sounds almost willfully euphemistic. More fundamentally, it appears, U.S. society has simply become deranged.

My sense—impressionistic, no doubt—is that the Italians I know and have lunched with over these past two years, whether, say, an academic historian (like me), a doctor, a grocery store clerk, an architect, or a retired construction foreman, have a different kind of investment in politics than most of the Americans I know—truth be told, a more highly educated and wealthy set, many of whom appear to have been positively consumed by the histrionics of recent U.S. politics.

Might we be better served if we had more rituals comparable to lunchtime in Italy? Specifically, might U.S. politics be better served?

Not because it would mean we would care less about politics, but rather because—by providing some respite from its storms—it would mean we could care less frantically, perhaps more productively. But dangers lurk here, too. Machiavelli, a Florentine, argued as forcefully as anyone that, for a republic to flourish, its members must not withdraw into their private lives. They must practice public *virtù*. They must care about politics. Without good politics, in the end, they cannot enjoy the good life (no matter what there is for lunch). But just how much should one care about politics, and what kind of caring are we talking about?

THE PERSONAL INTERSECTS OBLIQUELY with the political. Italians can be passionate about politics, of course, and not only from the fascist right. There are rich leftist traditions, from Antonio Gramsci to *operaismo* ("workerism"), Wages for Housework, and anti-Soviet Eurocommunism. But for all this, Italians may be better than Americans at finding, or perhaps inheriting, better ways to cope with political crisis in their private lives. That does not mean they have figured everything out. On the contrary, the country has faced its own three-decade political crisis, which only keeps groaning on.

The current Italian government is what is called a "technical" one. When a parliamentary majority formed after the 2018 general elections collapsed in 2021, the president of the republic appointed the former European Central Bank president Mario Draghi as the new prime minister. His mandate was to form a nonpartisan, national unity government to carry the country over until the next constitutionally mandated general election of 2023. Draghi ruled the country having never once faced an election.

Most every narrative I know for how Italian politics ended up here begins with the *tangentopoli* ("kickback city") corruption scandal of the early 1990s, which felled Italy's "First Republic," founded after World War II. Leading national politicians were disgraced, and some went to jail or fled the country. The center-left Social Democrats and center-right Christian Democrats, who had taken turns ruling the country after fascism, collapsed. After the fall of the Berlin Wall the Italian Communist Party, historically the largest and most influential in Western Europe, voted itself out of existence.

From these ashes arose media mogul Silvio Berlusconi, who first became prime minister in 1994. A genuine premonition of Trump, he formed a party around himself, and Italian politics became about Berlusconi, including his reputedly sex-crazed private life. In this respect, the 1990s in Italy and the United States were much the same: a decade that "slowly chipped away at the division between public and private," in the later words of Monica Lewinsky. But in other ways, personal and social life up until then in Italy was highly politicized. Which café or bar one frequented, which football club one rooted for, had ideological stakes.

After all, Gramsci's theory of hegemony had it that everyday culture must be conquered first, before the halls of the state. The Italian left took that teaching to heart. With the rise of Berlusconi—who, much like Trump after him, condemned leftist infiltration of the country's cultural institutions, from its universities to its television stations—at first all this intensified. My wife, a university student in Rome during some of these years, recalls many a lunch back then in which friends shouted at each other over politics, and sometimes ceased to be friends.

In the Berlusconi years, Italian politics appeared full of action. But nothing much really happened. Ultimately, many Italians became ever more aloof from politics, with bad results. In the end, very little was done to move the country in any direction. In recent decades, average Italian incomes have declined. The history of the Second Republic is one of aimless drift.

In 2011, during the European austerity crisis, the world's bond owners dumped so much Italian public debt that the Italian political class had to shuffle Berlusconi off stage. He went quietly enough, after having been prime minster for eleven out of the last seventeen years. Arguably, Italian politics has still not moved on from Berlusconi. A short-lived "technical government" collapsed in 2013, amidst the sudden rise of the antiestablishment Five Star Movement. The 2014 prime ministry of the youthful centrist Matteo Renzi lasted but two years. Berlusconi-like, in 2021 Renzi fled the center-left party, which he had once led in power, and formed a personal party of his own as he worked behind the scenes to help maneuverer Draghi into office.

In power, Draghi has increased state spending, drawing from European Union injections of cash. Recently he addressed a group of Italian students: "The pessimist accomplishes nothing and is only sad. You have to be in the future to win it. Enjoy yourselves!" But not long ago, over lunch in Bologna in the Piazza Aldrovandi with an Italian colleague, I asked her what, if anything, Draghi's public investment programs have accomplished so far. She smiled, and waved her hand: "Do you see anything new?" Plates of *tagliatelle al ragù,* a regional specialty, arrived, and we dropped the matter. For better or worse, Italians seem to know how and when to do this—how to compensate for present and future anxieties by taking solace in quotidian continuities with the distant past. When she waved at the Piazza Aldrovandi, I saw strikingly beautiful fourteenth-century buildings. Legend has it tagliatelle dates to the late 1400s.

This summer, in late July, as our family began to make our preparations to finally return to the United States, the Five Star pulled out of Draghi's government, suddenly plunging Italian politics back into crisis. Berlusconi, who still heads his own party, joined a vote of no confidence in the government, which collapsed. Draghi resigned as prime minister and is now a caretaker only. A snap election will be held early this fall. If current polls are any guide, the next Italian prime minister may well be Georgia Meloni, of the *Fratelli Italiani* (Brothers of Italy), a far-right party that has never before been in power, and which descends from Mussolini's fascists.

PERHAPS ITALIANS TAKE too much solace from leaning on the past. "Nobody can take politics seriously who does not hope to make things better for future generations": those are the words of the late American philosopher Richard Rorty. A case can be made that reveling in lunch is something to do to pass the time when one has cynically abandoned public life altogether—a way of "opting out," as Rorty put it, "becoming an ironic spectator of the nation rather than a participant in its political life."

Recalling these reflections lately, I decided to reread Rorty, an easier task given the recent publication of a collection of his popular political essays, *What Can We Hope For?* (2021). Rorty died in 2007, but after Trump was elected, his writings resurfaced due to a prophetic passage in his book *Achieving Our Century: Leftist Thought in Twentieth-Century America* (1998) that predicted U.S. politics might soon succumb to a right-wing demagogue should socioeconomic inequality increase and leftists focus exclusively on "cultural politics," by which he meant the politics of identity. I dimly recalled his arguments about an appropriate "split" in our moral lives between public and private, remembering it had something to do, in Rorty's philosophy, with issues of goodness and aesthetics, as well as, in his view, Americans' unique orientation to the future and dismissal of the past.

I went back to a passage in *Against Bosses, Against Oligarchs: A Conversation with Richard Rorty* (1998) called "Private and Public," which revisits Rorty's treatment of the same topic in his book *Contingency, Irony, and Solidarity* (1989). Rorty defends himself against his many left critics at that time, stating:

> The original misinterpretation came from Nancy Fraser, who said, 'Rorty didn't realize the personal is political.' I think she and I were at cross purposes. I was thinking of one sense of private, something like Whitehead's definition of religion: 'what you do with your solitude.' Fraser was thinking of the private as the kitchen or bedroom, as opposed to the marketplace and the office. There was no relevance to what I was saying.

There is relevance to what I am saying, however. Lunch is cooked in a kitchen. Rorty's interlocutor responds, "I can understand keeping your will toward self-creation private if you're Nietzsche."

(Friedrich Nietzsche, as it happens, was a passionate admirer of the Piedmont Italian city of Turin, where he settled and wrote both *Twilight of the Idols: Or How To Philosophize with a Hammer* [1889] and his last book, the autobiographical *Ecce Homo: How One Becomes What One Is* [1908], before succumbing to insanity. In a chapter in *Ecce Homo* titled "Why I Am So Clever," Nietzsche states that, "the 'salvation of humanity' depends to a far greater degree than it does upon any piece of theological curiosity: I refer to nutrition." He concludes, after a lengthy culinary digression, that "German intellect is indigestion" while "the best cooking is that of Piedmont.")

"What do you say," the question is next put to Rorty, "to the person whose sense of poetic self-creation requires other people and the opportunity for public transformation?" Rorty responds: "I would tell her to go into politics. I didn't say everybody had a public/private split, but some people do. There is a spectrum here. Some people have no public consciousness. This is the case of the sociopath; he simply doesn't think that there are any moral subjects out there." Rorty continues: "My public/private distinction wasn't an explanation of what every human life is like. I was, instead, urging that there was nothing wrong with letting people divide their lives along the private/public line. We don't have a moral responsibility to bring the two together."

Perhaps I am simply one of those humans with a public/private split. In my private life, after two years in Italy, I have come personally to value Italian-style lunchtime a lot. According to Rorty, I need not feel too guilty about this—nor should I, according to Fraser, if I am carrying an equal burden of the labor that goes into its preparation and into the cleaning up afterward. Although, all the better that I do feel guilty. This is evidence that I do have a "public consciousness," and that my passion for lunchtime is not—at least, not yet—sociopathic.

And yet, something about Rorty's argument is not completely satisfying. "Moral responsibility to bring them together," no—but do we not all have a need to integrate, however minimally, our different selves, including our many public and private selves, into the same working psyche? When we do not, perhaps our public and private selves both suffer the worse for it, and perhaps this part of what has gone wrong with U.S. life lately.

I HAD NOT READ RORTY in a decade. Over that time, not only had *What Can We Hope For?* come out, but so had *Pragmatism as Anti-Authoritarianism* (2021), an edited series of ten lectures that Rorty gave in Spain in 1996. At the high tide of late twentieth-century globalization, Rorty traveled to Europe, where he fully spelled out for the last time his mature version of the most self-consciously "American" philosophical project.

In the first lecture, Rorty states his theme: that the great American pragmatists of the turn of the twentieth century—William James and John Dewey—should be read as completing the Enlightenment project of antiauthoritarianism. They did that, Rorty argues, by extending the Enlightenment political critique of absolute sovereignty to epistemology and metaphysics. If there are no good reasons to submit to kings, then there are no better reasons to submit to a nonhuman, capital-R "Reality," or a capital-T "Truth" independent of ourselves. Deep "rational foundations" to liberal democracy do not exist, Rorty holds. There are only uncertain political projects, occurring in the stream of Darwinian evolution, that either make human life better or worse. They make life better, Rorty argues, not if they correspond to eternal, universal truths, like abstract principles of justice, but rather if they diminish suffering and generate social institutions that humiliate no one, making possible greater happiness in the future. This happens through projects of individual self-creation but also through community. For once we abandon commitments to things like timeless reality, and swap out eternity for futurity, we find we are only left with ourselves and with one another—not with Truth, but sensate emotional attachments to living, breathing communities.

But all this poses an obvious question. Why didn't Enlightenment thinkers go all the way themselves, completing their own project? To answer this question, the first lecture makes a sharp turn halfway through. Rorty creatively explores a resonance between pragmatism and what he calls one of Sigmund Freud's "wacky" books, *Moses and Monotheism* (1939). In it, Freud presents a genealogy of civilizational progress, first found in his *Totem and Taboo* (1913), by which social cooperation first emerged from parricide. In this story, a band of brothers murdered their "primal father," a domineering figure with unchecked power over the community. To ritualistically distribute his power among them, the fraternal alliance gathered for a grand feast and cannibalized the murdered primal father for their meal. (Was it for lunch? Freud does not say, though according to one biographer, lunch was Freud's "main meal" of the day.)

Afterward, the fraternal alliance, feeling guilty and rudderless and hoping to banish the memory of their deed, decided to sacralize the primal father's memory in a physical totem, which they began to anxiously idolize and worship. Later, Freud speculated, monotheism simply replaced idolatry with God worship. Rorty supplements Freud by adding that Platonism replaced Hellenic polytheism with the worship of timeless, perfect Ideas, including the "Idea of the Good," discoverable by Reason. The Enlightenment, drawing from Platonism, in the end replaced God worship with Reason and Truth worship. However strongly psychologically motivated, this was nonetheless a philosophical and political mistake. Thus Nietzsche, whom Rorty saw as a philosophical if not political ally, recommended focusing upon the significance of nutrition and not theology—the all-too-human scale of lunchtime, that is, rather than eternal Truth.

According to Rorty, much of Western philosophy can be interpreted as a defense formation, intellectualized as "metaphysics", which expresses unconscious yearnings for a lost parent to love, as Rorty puts it, "with all one's heart and soul and strength." Only pragmatism "reaps the full advantages of parricide," he thinks, by celebrating "fraternity freed from memory of paternal authority." Rorty remarks that the debates of his lifetime in philosophy about "realism," and even the broader culture about "Truth," were debates between "two types of people" describable in Freudian terms: "the type of people who are still subject to the need to ally themselves with an authority-figure and those who are untroubled by this need." In other words, those who integrate their psyches around a fixed point of authority and certainty, and those who simply do not feel the need.

We are almost back to lunch. Supporting the above claims, Rorty draws another contrast—between the beautiful and the sublime. Whereas the sublime is unrepresentable, indescribable, and ineffable— like Plato's Idea of the Good, the God of monotheism, or Reality in modern Western metaphysics—"a merely beautiful object or state of affairs unifies a manifold in an especially satisfying way." Whereas "the beautiful harmonizes finite things with other finite things," by contrast the "sublime escapes finitude, and therefore both unity and plurality." Whereas "to contemplate the beautiful is to contemplate something manageable, something which consists of recognizable parts put together in recognizable ways," "to be swept away by the sublime is to be carried beyond both recognition and description."

In this scheme, lunch may be beautiful, sublime, or neither. A lunch that unifies a manifold in an especially satisfying way could well be beautiful—*bello*, as Italians would call it, a word they use not only for objects and places but also experiences and states of being. But, if in their solitude one wants to know what a particularly delicious mozzarella is, as a thing-in-and-of-itself, by striving to know it by tasting it, and to be swept away by the sublime experience beyond description, then one certainly has the right. Should one find lunchtime companions so motivated, no problem there, either—you have started a new religion. Or perhaps lunch holds no value for you whatsoever. That is fine, too.

Rorty's point is that we must not look for sublime experiences in public life. Or, if we do, this will always involve the powerful forcing the powerless to submit to their version of the sublime, the Good— their description of timeless, universal truths. We should only try for the beautiful. That is enough. Note here, how small the political gains of anti-Trump liberals have been when defending "the Truth" amidst Trump's lies, while how central the word "beautiful" has been to the success of Trump's political rhetoric. ("Build that big, beautiful wall.")

What Can One Hope For? pleads again and again with leftists to come up with beautiful new descriptions of what a future "global cooperative commonwealth" might one day be like. The foretelling of Trump in *Achieving Our Country* has led some to see Rorty as a prophet of political doom. This gets him exactly wrong. His political sensibility was in fact very much of his times: the late twentieth century, an era of optimism after the end of the Cold War, when democracy was triumphantly on the global march, before *Bush v. Gore*, 9/11, the war in Iraq, Hurricane Katrina, and the Great Recession. In the 1990s Rorty tried his best to pick up the mantle of James, Dewey, Walt Whitman, Ralph Waldo Emerson, and Abraham Lincoln to fashion a philosophically anti-foundationalist rhetoric of "social hope" in the homespun idiom of American pragmatism. Reading his popular political writings collected in *What Can We Hope For?* more than two decades later is like reading Barack Obama's 2008 campaign speeches.

It is hard to know whether to be inspired by the hortatory political optimism or to grimace at the naiveté. Nowadays it is hard to be so optimistic. Recently, over lunch in the Trastevere neighborhood of Rome with my family visiting from Texas, it was my twelve-year-old nephew who, taking the measure of Europe for the first time, quipped to the family, "America is good for two things: racism and guns."

THOMAS AQUINAS WAS BORN in 1125 just outside Aquino, an area in the center of Italy that produces a genuinely sublime mozzarella. It is also the site of one of the deadliest battles of the Italian campaign during World War II, before the Allies bombed a German position at Mount Cassino, destroying a hilltop abbey that dated back to 539. It was Aquinas who said that God, and only God, can see the past, present, and future in a single vision. That is the one truly sublime perspective, which has no business informing our shared, public life, according to Rorty.

We cannot see the past, present, and future all at once, so we live torn among them.

One of Freud's most powerful insights was that, in practice, psychic integration cannot help but to revolve around rituals of repetition. Regarding politics, in particular, we might wonder about the degree to which repetitions veer toward pathology—both individually and collectively. Are we suffering in private, scrolling Twitter a thousand times a day and calling it politics? Or are we taking private pleasure in the daily enjoyment of communal practices, while at the same time engaging in the repetitive tasks of building social movements for greater justice?

Morally speaking, Rorty was correct that one of political liberalism's great strengths is that it treats the public and private as realms that do not need to be unified into the same metaphysical whole, yet he was wrong to picture public and private ideally as "split," because they do require practical, working integration in the spaces of our individual and collective psyche. If all liberal democracies must face the problem of where to draw the line between public and private, then a no less important task is to integrate them, while somehow still holding them distant. For this to happen, there must be practices through which the temporalities of private and public life, keeping their margins, nonetheless meet in communal life.

Even if just as an aspiration, lunchtime in Italy does this. It is a private matter, distant enough from politics. But the rituals of its practice, from the rhythms of its pacing to the standard recipes that one does not meddle with, are shared public goods inherited from the past, as tangible as the country's architectural patrimony. They maintain a minimal, baseline solidarity in civic life.

Society holds. One marks time with friends, family, strangers, and comrades, waiting for the next political opening—to build a better future for all. We cannot know when, but the moment will come around in Italy, and it will come around in the United States, too. Let us hope that it will be soon.

PLEASURABLE WORK, PLENTIFUL LEISURE: WILLIAM MORRIS'S SOCIALIST VISION

Ben Schacht

"APART FROM THE DESIRE to produce beautiful things," declared British designer, printer, and artist William Morris in his 1894 essay "How I Became a Socialist," "the leading passion in my life has been and is hatred of modern civilization."

Morris cast a skeptical eye on his era's triumphant claims to social and technological progress. Born on the cusp of the Victorian age to well-to-do parents in 1834, Morris attended Oxford and befriended Dante Gabriel Rossetti and other members of the Pre-Raphaelite Brotherhood before pursuing his leading passions in a remarkable array of literary and artistic endeavors.

Prior to embracing socialism in the early 1880s, Morris was a painter and a respected poet—author of such works as *The Defense of Guenevere* (1858) and *The Earthly Paradise* (1868)—a prolific designer of household goods at his firm Morris and Co., and a campaigner for the protection of ancient buildings. In 1891, five years before his death, he founded the Kelmscott Press, which showcased his mastery of typography and the book arts. In addition to publishing exquisite editions of great works of English literature, such as Geoffrey Chaucer's *Canterbury Tales*, Morris wrote and published a series of prose romances which influenced the subsequent development of fantasy and science fiction, including the works of J. R. R. Tolkien and H. G. Wells.

While socialism remains an enduring aspect of Morris's legacy, his reputation today is based mainly on his artistic accomplishments—his enchanting, perennially popular wallpaper and textile designs above all—and his role as a founding figure of the Arts and Crafts movement in decorative arts, which rejected mass production and the industrial organization of labor in favor of the traditional handicraft techniques of the past. (His ideas about art and architecture would go on to influence prominent modernist designers, including members of the Bauhaus and Frank Lloyd Wright.)

Given Morris's avowed hatred of modern civilization and his artistic immersion in the subjects and materials of bygone ages, it might be tempting to wave away his socialism as little more than a nostalgic denunciation of industrial progress in the name of an idealized depiction of the medieval craftsman. In reality, Morris's socialism was rigorous and revolutionary, influenced as much by Karl Marx as by John Ruskin and Thomas Carlyle, the two Victorian social critics from whom he learned to doubt his era's reigning ideology of progress. Morris was clear-eyed about the oppressions of the past, precise in his criticisms of the present, and optimistic about the ability of the broad mass of workers to replace the misery, alienation, and ugliness he observed in late Victorian Britain with a mode of life and labor conducive to joy and beauty—a future he depicted in his 1890 utopian novel *News from Nowhere*.

Far from anachronistic, his vision of socialism as a globe-spanning cooperative society based on freely undertaken, creative, ecologically sustainable work remains an urgent alternative to the present system of overwork, environmental destruction, and nationalist rivalry that currently threatens our health, sanity, and indeed our very existence. At a moment of profound struggle over the future of work, amid concatenating crises of climate change and democratic decline, Morris's body of work is worth recovering for its radical vision of ways of living that prioritize pleasure and beauty for all.

MORRIS SPELLS OUT the deep connections between art and socialism in numerous writings, describing the threat capitalism poses to art by undermining people's living and working conditions. He has little patience for those who would separate art from everyday life. "Any one who professes to think that the question of art and cultivation must go before that of the knife and fork," he proclaims in "How I Became a Socialist," "does not understand what art means, or how that its roots must have a soil of thriving and unanxious life."

This declaration crystallizes views on the nature of art that Morris had begun expressing in public in the 1870s, before his turn toward "practical socialism." Fed up with "ministering to the swinish luxuries of the rich," who formed the core of his design firm's clientele, Morris declared that he did "not want art for a few, any more than education for a few, or freedom for a few." Consequently, he championed a democratic concept of art in which beauty was accessible to everyone. In "Art Under Plutocracy," a lecture he delivered in 1883, Morris pleads for a more expansive definition of art in which its meaning is extended

> beyond those matters which are consciously works of art, to take in not only painting and sculpture, and architecture, but the shapes and colors of all household goods, nay, even the arrangement of the fields for tillage and pasture, the management of towns and of our highways of all kinds; in a word, to extend to the aspect of the externals of our life.

Morris's views on art and beauty were strongly influenced by Ruskin, who argued in his 1853 book *The Stones of Venice* that the worker of the nineteenth century was deprived of the liberty, freedom of thought, and creative pleasure that the worker of the Middle Ages enjoyed—qualities that Ruskin saw expressed in the organic forms of Gothic architecture. (Morris published Ruskin's chapter "The Nature of the Gothic" as a standalone Kelmscott edition in 1892.) According to Ruskin, the workers of the industrial age suffer not because they are merely "ill fed" but because "the degradation of the operative into a machine" means that "they have no pleasure in the work by which they make their bread." Industrial civilization prides itself on its "invention of the division of labor," says Ruskin, "only we give it a false name. It is not, truly speaking, the labor that is divided; but the men:—Divided into mere segments of men—broken into small fragments and crumbs of life."

Morris often argues in this vein. "Art," he contends, "is man's expression of his joy in labor." It follows from this definition that an unartistic society is one in which labor has been deprived of its joyful and artistic qualities. Hence the "chief accusation" that Morris launches "against the modern state of society is that it is founded on the art-lacking or unhappy labour of the greater part of men."

For Morris the problem was not merely that industrial methods of production had replaced the techniques of the medieval craftsman, leading to low-quality, mass-produced goods and the deskilling of labor. It was that this rise of machinery hadn't liberated workers from grueling toil. In fact, Morris explicitly rejected the proposition that machinery itself was to blame for the degradation of work, looking to deeper social causes as the true explanation. He does argue that the medieval "system of a man working for himself leisurely and happily was infinitely better, both as regards the worker and his work, than that division of labor system which the profit-grinding of rising commercialism supplanted it by." But he also recognizes that "it is impossible to go back to such a simple system, even if it would not involve, as it would, a return to the whole hierarchical, or feudal state of society."

Rather than looking backward, Morris looks forward to the abolition of class and hierarchy altogether. His close reading of Marx's *Capital*—which Morris, who did not read German, read in the first French edition of 1875—leads him to locate the art-destroying properties of capitalism not in machine production as such but in the social purposes to which such production is put: namely, the pursuit of profit.

Though there is a long-running scholarly debate about the extent of Morris's Marxism, his use of Marxist concepts to explain the incompatibility of capitalism with art are evident throughout his socialist period. In "Attractive Labor," for example, an article that Morris published in the *Commonweal* in 1885, he writes:

> The creation of surplus value being the one aim of the employers of labor, they cannot for a moment trouble themselves as to whether the work which creates that surplus value is pleasurable to the worker or not. In fact in order to get the greatest amount of surplus value out of the work, and to make a profit in the teeth of competition, it is absolutely necessary that it be done under such conditions as make . . . a mere burden which nobody would endure unless upon compulsion.

The systemic compulsion to work for wages—"the fear of death by starvation" which is the worker's "only motive to exertion"—and the lack of art go together, according to Morris: the "absence of pleasure is the second gift to the world which the development of commercialism has added to its first gift of a propertyless proletariat." It is this division of society into propertied and propertyless classes that must be overcome if art is to be revived, Morris contends. His vision of a socialist future in which art flourishes is therefore one in which wage labor has been abolished:

> When people are not working for wages, but for the wealth of the community: the work would be done deliberately and thoughtfully for the good's sake and not for profit's sake. . . . Work so done, with variety and intelligently, not intensified to the bursting point of the human machine, and yet with real workmanlike, or rather artistic eagerness, would not be a burden but an interest added to life quite apart from its necessity.

Schacht

As this passage suggests, Morris has a nuanced view of work. On the one hand, he desires to make the experience of work better—more artistic, more "pleasurable." Liberated from the imperatives of capitalist labor, work would cease to be a "burden" and become "an interest added to life" rather than a mechanism for the satisfaction of basic needs. This is comparable to the attitude expressed by Marx in *The Critique of the Gotha Program* (1875), which describes communism as the state in which "labor has ceased to be a burden and has become life's prime want"—no longer simply a means to an end but an end in itself.

On the other hand, Morris's belief that we can make work pleasurable—something we positively and freely desire to do—does not lead him to lose sight of the need for leisure and a life outside of work. "The leisure which Socialism above all things aims at obtaining for the worker," he writes, "is also the very thing that breeds desire—desire for beauty, for knowledge, for more abundant life, in short." He predicts that with the advent of socialism, the use of machinery for communal purposes and the equal distribution of work will mean that "much less labor will be necessary for each workman . . . so that the working time of each member of our factory will be very short, say . . . four hours a day."

Limiting the duration of work was fundamental to Morris's conception of artistic labor. One of the three constitutive elements of what Morris calls "useful work" is "the hope of rest." "When class-robbery is abolished," Morris writes in *Useful Work versus Useless Toil* (1884), "every man will reap the fruits of his labor, every man will have due rest—leisure, that is." While there can be no doubt that Morris prized useful, creative work, there are clear affinities between his praise of leisure and the attitude of his *Commonweal* colleague Paul Lafargue, whose 1883 book *The Right to Be Lazy* is one of the ur-texts of today's anti-work politics. Indeed, the subtitle of *News from Nowhere*—"an epoch of rest"—testifies to the primacy of leisure in Morris's vision of the good life under socialism.

IF THE FLOURISHING OF ART through the overcoming of wage labor was one pillar of Morris's socialist vision, another was his resolute internationalism—an attitude that remains as relevant today as it was during Morris's time.

Morris's commitment to international solidarity is especially evident in the activism he undertook as a member of the Socialist League, which was formed in 1885 after splitting off from Henry Hyndman's Social Democratic Federation due to irreconcilable disputes over personality and ideology. Along with Eleanor Marx, Karl's youngest daughter, Morris helped to steer the organization toward a politics based on the solidarity of all workers, wherever they happened to hail from. This principle was clearly articulated in the Socialist League's manifesto, which appeared in the first issue of the *Commonweal*, the League's print organ, in 1885:

> For us neither geographical boundaries, political history, race, nor creed makes rivals or enemies; for us there are no nations, but only varied masses of workers and friends, whose mutual sympathies are checked or perverted by groups of masters and fleecers whose interest it is to stir up rivalries and hatreds between the dwellers in different lands.

Schacht

Morris's internationalism abounds in such pieces as "How We Live and How We Might Live," in which he declares that "our present system of Society is based on a state of perpetual war":

> As nations under the present system are driven to compete with one another for the markets of the world, and as firms or the captains of industry have to scramble for their share of the profits of the markets, so also have the workers to compete with each other—for livelihood; and it is this constant competition or war amongst them which enables the profit-grinders to make their profits, and by means of wealth so acquired to take all the executive power of the country into their hands.

Indeed, racial and nationalist rivalries only serve to hinder the unity of the working class, in Morris's view, distracting from the principal antagonism between capital and labor. This point is especially clear in his writings on the Irish and Italian movements for national independence, "Ireland and Italy: A Warning." "For my part," writes Morris, "I do not believe in the race-hatred of the Irish against the English: they hate their English *masters*, as well they may; and their English masters are now trying hard to stimulate the race-hatred among their English brethren, the workers, by all this loud talk of the integrity of Empire and so forth." He concludes with the general advice: "Your revolutionary struggles will be abortive or lead to mere disappointment unless you accept as your watchword, WAGE-WORKERS OF ALL COUNTRIES UNITE!"

Morris was animated not only by a sense of solidarity with workers around the world but also by a profound concern for the Earth itself. He was a prescient observer of capitalism's ecological destructiveness. Born at the dawn of the age of fossil capital—to borrow Andreas Malm's term for the complex of social and economic forces that drove the transition to steam-powered factories—Morris was one of the first to articulate connections between overwork, the waste created by the drive for profit, and pollution. At a time when "progress" was in vogue, he was among a group of radical Victorians who called attention to the environmental risks posed by unregulated commercial industry. He stresses not just the technological means but also the social motives at play in the destruction of the environment. "It is profit," he writes—he does not blame merely machinery or industry—that wraps "a whole district in a cloud of sulphureous smoke; which turns beautiful rivers into filthy sewers."

Accordingly, his vision of a better world emphasizes its natural beauty. When William Guest, the protagonist of *News from Nowhere*, wakes up in the socialist society of the future, he is surprised by the clarity of the Thames and its scenic, placid banks: "The soap works with their smoke-vomiting chimneys were gone; the engineer's works gone; the lead works gone; and no sound of riveting and hammering came down the west wind from Thorneycroft's."

TO SOME Morris's ideas may sound naively idealistic—utopian in the pejorative sense. But as a revolutionary socialist, he did not eschew questions of strategy; in fact he discusses them explicitly in various writings, all of which abound in wariness of parliamentary politics. In "The Policy of Abstention," for example, Morris argues that socialists ought not to engage in parliamentary politics but should instead agitate among the masses and organize an alternative labor parliament. And in "Whigs, Democrats and Socialists," he cautions that while it may be permissible for socialists to enter parliament for purposes of disrupting it, they must resist being seduced into the business of parliament and enacting palliative measures that serve only to perpetuate capitalist class rule by making it marginally more tolerable.

Whatever one makes of his strategic views, Morris's critique of capitalism endures because of his intense focus on alienated work— which remains as potent a source of mental, physical, and ecological destructiveness as it was in Morris's times. Indeed, as E. P. Thompson put it, Morris is "our greatest diagnostician of alienation." His distinctive politics of pleasure aimed above all to liberate workers from the soul-destroying depredations of wage labor, giving them more time and freedom to enjoy the activities that make life worth living. That is a politics we desperately need to revive today.

THE UTOPIAN PULSE
Lynne Segal

MOST OF US have struggled to maintain our mental well-being throughout the COVID-19 pandemic. Surrounded by fear and apprehension, it's been hard to keep hope alive. In my experience, those who have managed to find ways to feel useful have fared better than most. I was lucky: well before the sudden appearance of COVID-19, I had already been writing about our shared forms of vulnerability, global interdependencies, and the need to place the complexities of care at the very heart of politics. Even timelier, four friends had joined me to study our culture's historic refusal to value care work. Our resulting small Care Collective quickly produced a book for Verso, *The Care Manifesto* (2020), keeping us all busier than ever, as we connected with others around the world who were also addressing the politics of care. As we developed our vision of a truly caring world, we focused on how governments, municipalities, and media outlets might become more caring, working to promote collective joy rather than their current narrow and duplicitous concern with individual aspiration, knowing that so many will inescapably flounder. Understanding that we all depend on each other, and nurturing rather than denying our interdependencies, encourages us all to work to cultivate a world in which each of us can not only live, but thrive.

Such ambitions return me to the political milieu I encountered as a young adult in the 1960s. Young Australian radicals then were aware that appalling events were happening around the globe, but they rarely reached our doorstep, least of all in my "lucky" birthplace of Sydney. "Lucky," that is, for its incoming settlers over the previous two centuries who barely registered the genocide of the country's indigenous inhabitants, the Aboriginal people and Torres Strait Islanders. We did hear about the Sharpeville Massacre in 1960, with anti-Apartheid struggles often drawing us onto the streets in boisterous protest outside the South African embassy. By the close of the decade, however, we were rallying regularly outside U.S. embassies, with opposition to the Vietnam War quickly the imprimatur of progressive consciousness.

Optimism flourished on many fronts throughout the decade. Calls to "Make Love, Not War" rang around the world, and the graffiti adorning Parisian walls during the flashpoint of 1960s protest told us to believe anything was possible: "Be Realistic, Demand the Impossible," "Live Without Dead Time," "Form Dream Committees." Calls for hedonistic revolt reverberated, reaching even far-off Sydney. These calls were always laced with the thrill of unfettered sexual freedom. "We must make love / Instead of making money," urged the gleeful British playwright and poet Adrian Mitchell. In 1968 the Beatles song "Revolution" entered the Top 20 charts in the anglophone world. "We all want to change the world," they sang, calling for evolutionary and nonviolent change. Meanwhile, the term "sexism" was coined during that decade, as male braggadocio burgeoned at the barricades despite so many passionate young women joining the protests. These lively years of movement politics, awash with collective joys and occasional tears, would soon launch women's liberation as its first and most persisting progeny.

Indeed, the spirit of the sixties was the cradle of women's liberation, which would be encompassed in second-wave feminism in the seventies. During that decade, ideas from the earlier New Left's Herbert Marcuse, Raymond Williams, Edward Thompson, and Stuart Hall were imbibed with possibilities for critical engagement with the good life. Hall, the most charismatic of the New Left thinkers, became the founding editor of *New Left Review* in 1960 and set the journal's early utopian tone. Quoting the archetypal nineteenth-century visionary William Morris, he called for the creation of a "society of equals," where people no longer needed to escape immiseration but had the resources to pursue meaningful, pleasurable lives. "Life is something *lived*," he wrote, "not something one passes through like tea through a strainer." Thompson, a Marxist historian and later leading peace campaigner, was also determined to put Morris back on the left's reading list, with hopes of achieving a new alliance between socialism and utopianism. Like French philosopher Miguel Abensour, Thompson argued that Morris's goal was the "education of desire," urging us to desire differently and reject the purely commercial reasoning of capitalism. These male mentors all spoke of the significance of culture and community life, alongside support for civil rights, while applauding calls for direct action and cross-class solidarity. It was into this heady mix that budding feminist voices placed women's subordination, incorporating questions of intimacy and community life at the center of politics.

Nowhere did this happen faster than in the United States. As one of its iconic chroniclers, Alix Kates Shulman, wrote in *Burning Questions* (1978), her semi-fictionalized memoir of women's awakening in the sixties, "I find myself happier than I ever dreamed I could be." She wasn't alone. The ardent optimism of that time, expressed by Sheila Rowbotham, Ellen Willis, Adrienne Rich, and Audre Lorde, quickly joined by the voices of thousands of women globally, seemed to suggest that the space between desiring change and realizing it was shrinking. And there were many victories, however short-lived some proved: new laws supported women's rights and equality in the home and workplace, alongside a growing cultural acceptance of women's reproductive autonomy.

Antiracist struggles were occurring simultaneously, as the civil rights movement in the United States had for years influenced U.S. activists. Millions of Black people had listened to Martin Luther King, Jr.'s legendary speech "I Have a Dream" during the March on Washington in 1963, demanding civil and economic rights for African Amercians. Though it never proved easy to unite across class divides and diverse "identity struggles," the collective effervescence of such varied rebellion provoked deep-rooted conservative panic, which explains why the sixties and its legacies have been trashed in conservative retellings.

LOOKING BACK TODAY, we seem so very far from the spirit of jubilation that energized those street-fighting years. It was perhaps best captured by the words of charismatic British Trotskyist Tariq Ali, who placed this bold proclamation on the front page of the first edition of *The Black Dwarf* in 1968: "WE SHALL FIGHT, WE WILL WIN, PARIS, LONDON, ROME, BERLIN."

After sixty years of consistently engaging in radical thought and action—picket lines, marches, and fervent writing—it's daunting to see that we now face a world that looks more unequal and uncaring than ever. It's a glum outlook for progressives of any stripe. Progress and improvements for some is matched by continuing poverty and decline for many others. Once we add the impact of a global pandemic and an overheating planet, it's clear why dystopian scenarios have become more seductive than ever.

Yet the recent combination of COVID-19, worsening climate crises, and other calamities *did* also convince more people that something is drastically wrong with a system in which many of us no longer have the time or resources to care adequately for each other or for the world at large. The result is two radical imaginations pushing in deeply contrasting directions.

For some, we are finally leaving behind the mayhem of capitalism, but only for something even worse. The entrenchment of unregulated corporations is threatening to sideline the state and render workers' struggles futile. After seeing the trillions the U.S. government handed out to corporations during the COVID-19 pandemic with no strings attached, Marxist historian Robert Brenner concluded in the *New Left Review*, "What we have had for a long epoch is worsening economic decline met by intensifying political predation." Similarly, witnessing the widespread acceleration of workers into precarious gig economies, with digital platforms amassing free data from us all, Greek economist Yanis Varoufakis insists that we are now living in a postcapitalist, techno-feudalist dystopia. Building on the work of Marxist feminist McKenzie Wark, Jodi Dean also asserts that capitalism has reverted to a form of "neo-feudalism," with the extreme wealth of the few reliant upon a perpetually precarious, impoverished underclass.

For those not resolutely blind to the suffering of others, such thinking resonates with our awareness of the difficulties and despair of so many who are deprived of any sense of control over their lives. Yet such pessimism can dangerously align us with a form of reactionary conservatism, merely gawping at the dire state of things, apparently helpless before impending disaster. This dystopian imagination has hovered around popular culture for decades, with any form of utopian yearning all but obliterated in fantasies of frightful futures: Hollywood offers us visions of a wasteland where teenage Amazons compete and die (The Hunger Games, 2012–15), a United States in which half the human race is enslaved as breeders (*The Handmaid's Tale*, 2017–22), and a society in which disposable people are bred for their body parts to be harvested by the rich (*Never Let Me Go*, 2010).

Such scenarios at least partially mirror a reality where unrestrained corporate power has been allowed to invade much of the former public sector, enabling rocketing inequality, government corruption, police brutality, rising racism, and fatal cruelties toward refugees and the vulnerable. Such market fundamentalism has encouraged an uber-individualism dismissive of weakness, one that disavows our basic human interdependence or need to preserve the planet on which we all depend.

Yet this market mindset has never gone unchallenged, least of all in recent years, during which we have seen growing calls for collective resistance to our governments' capitulations to corporate interests. Like other progressive activists trying to stay buoyant today, I often borrow Raymond Williams's 1980 reminder in *New Left Review* that radical politics must be about "making hope possible, rather than despair convincing."

This year, in *Taking Control! Humanity and America After Trump and the Pandemic* (2022), English writer and campaigner Anthony Barnett offers his own tempered optimism for sustaining progressive, democratic spirits. With Williams, Barnett served on the editorial board of *New Left Review,* and he praises the prescience of his old colleague on two points: first, for noting the necessity of aligning economic arguments with ecological ones, and, second, for warning against the urge to treat people as "available raw material" for profit. Like Williams, Barnett applauds the significance of feminism and attempts to shift away from an exclusive focus on market production. He instead advocates for a notion of "livelihood" to help us gain "confidence in *our own* energies and capacities."

Barnett draws hope from the surge in climate activism in recent years. He turns to the works of influential left economists—such as Kate Raworth's *Doughnut Economics* (2017), Thomas Piketty's *Capital in the Twenty-First Century* (2014), and Marianna Mazzucato's *The Value of Everything* (2018)—to suggest that more people are realizing that we must replace old commitments to endless growth with regimes prepared to invest in diverse forms of social and shared ownership, alongside ecological preservation. As Raworth spells out, wishing for constant growth is a planetary death wish. Instead we must create economies that promote a flourishing web of life for humans and the world at large.

WE REMAIN SO FAR from true human and nonhuman flourishing. This awareness triggered my recent involvement in producing *The Care Manifesto*, an appeal to address our continuing failure to value the crucial labor of care. Market logics lack the vocabulary to genuinely understand the complexities of caring, despite the many forms of "care-washing" smearing the packaging delivered by insecure, underpaid delivery workers.

Unlike commodity production, care work is not quantifiable. It is relational, and requires time, flexibility, and creativity. However rewarding and meaningful it might be, it is often challenging work that ideally ensures some reciprocal sense of agency and well-being between caregivers and receivers. Women were traditionally charged with supplying care work, but now most are in the paid workforce. Neither Britain nor the United States has passed any meaningful legislation acknowledging the care work women are often shouldered with providing; to the contrary, both countries have made substantial cuts to welfare provisions. These factors have combined to create an alarming care deficit. This gap has been largely filled by global care chains that exploit Black and migrant women. Thus, earlier feminist demands for the sharing of caring responsibilities, alongside the necessary resources and welfare provision to enrich our households and communities, are now more urgent than ever.

Much political energy is currently returning to centering these demands. We see it in the confident growth of the Global Women's Strike movement which calls attention to the universal failure to value care work. Indeed, women are mobilizing around the world, from the nationwide Polish women's strike against their government's 2016 attempts to criminalize abortion, to the tens of thousands of women in Argentina who took to the streets in 2015 to protest against femicide as part of the militant #NiUnaMenos (Not One Less) movement. And we see it happening now across the United States, as women take to the streets to protest the Supreme Court's overturning of *Roe v. Wade*.

There is hope—and joy—in this kind of collective action. For despite the neoliberal propaganda that we only have ourselves to rely on for our well-being, the opposite is true. More of us are becoming aware of the dishonesty behind the myth of self-reliance and self-fulfilment, when the rich and powerful always have an army of helpers at hand to serve them. We know that people are more likely to find pleasure and well-being through their encounters with others, in sharing their joys and sorrows whenever they can.

I wrote about the significance and pleasures of collectivity in *Radical Happiness: Moments of Collective Joy* (2017). There I drew upon Hannah Arendt's *On Revolution* (1963), in which she suggests that no one could be called either happy or free without feeling they had some ability to shape public power. For Arendt, it was only through public engagement that people might consolidate a feeling of democratic belonging, as well as what she called *amor mundi*, love of the world. Arendt valued a sense of agency that arises through collective action and deliberation. Judith Butler has often echoed this sentiment, stressing the importance of realizing a sense of public belonging through the possibilities available for participating in shared action and debate. Care theorist Joan Tronto agrees, albeit from a slightly different perspective. In her book *Caring Democracy* (2013), she argues that once we acknowledge that dependence is a fact of all our lives, freedom lies in our capacity to care for others and commit to who and what we care about.

The significance of caring and collective engagement was at the fore during the challenging years we just faced. Despite government and corporate failures to prioritize all the lives affected by the pandemic, especially globally, extraordinary grassroots action offered support to those most in need. Globally, mutual aid groups flourished. In the very first month of the virus, voluntary workers from all walks of life signed up to help those self-isolating. In the United Kingdom, millions of volunteers in local communities supported food banks, with many offering their time to tackle issues of homelessness, debt, and mental distress. Over the last decade, we have seen democratically run neighborhood forums and caring hubs spring up globally, helping communities to resist and survive austerity regimes. To be sure, these activities can help *all involved*; 2021 research at the London School of Economics (LSE) found that volunteering gave people a sense of purpose and pleasure, increasing their overall well-being.

It is in the United States, however—with its daunting levels of inequality, racism, police brutality, incarceration, and extreme suspicion of politicians—that grassroots activism has been most pronounced. When COVID-19 arrived in March 2020, widespread aid networks grew immensely in most major cities, with armies of volunteers raising money for those who needed help with food and rent. Researching these initiatives for her 2020 *New Yorker* essay "What Mutual Aid Can Do During a Pandemic," staff reporter Jia Tolentino pondered the origins and long-term significance of this extraordinary burst of solidarity and support, while herself active in aid networks on her doorstep in Brooklyn. However, knowing that feel-good stories can be leveraged by conservatives wishing to champion volunteerism over state welfare programs, Tolentino stressed that such projects would only survive in the long term if backed by public support. The researchers at LSE came to similar conclusions; volunteering and mutual aid need public funding to flourish in the long run.

Nevertheless, activist and perennial optimist Rebecca Solnit, covering the rise of mutual aid for the *Guardian* in May 2020, suggests that radical collective moments can sometimes manage to sustain enduring resistance and networking. For example, she references the Common Ground Health Clinic that formed in response to the devastation of Hurricane Katrina in New Orleans in 2005, which has managed to continue delivering free medical care for over fifteen years. With no foreseeable end to job losses from the pandemic, Solnit suggests that this sudden spread of generosity and solidarity foreshadows what is possible, and certainly necessary, for our future survival. Many volunteers may return "to normal," but some will retain a new awareness of who they are, their ties to others, and what matters most. We can renew our attachments to life by embracing its sorrows as well as its joys, which often feel far larger than our own concerns. Coming together in moments of collective fear and despair to work on common ground also enables moments of collective joy even with small victories.

THERE IS A CERTAIN ENERGY that comes with envisioning a more equitable, peaceful, and fairer world—and sharing such imaginings. Some psychologists, including Tim Kasser and Malte Klar, report links between political activism and feelings of well-being. Kasser and Klar interviewed hundreds of college students about their levels of political engagement, optimism, and overall happiness, finding that student activists showed greater signs of well-being than other college students. Their shared political work gave them a sense of purpose, meaning, and pleasure in life. Given that most young people today are experiencing some form of anxiety around climate change, climate activism—the feeling that one is acting to effect change and has agency in the face of disaster—can offer significant remedial benefits.

Eventually we will all find that our corporeal bodies fail us, and our desires will be frustrated or rejected. Yet our own miseries often recede when paying heed to the lives of others, as poet Adrienne Rich often noted, using her own experience of early-onset rheumatoid arthritis to unite her in solidarity with the suffering of others, with the "pain on the streets." Rich also spoke of the "radical" happiness she could share with others in moments of heightened political engagement. Similarly, another well-known American feminist, Lauren Berlant, argues in their influential book *Cruel Optimism* (2011) that "the political" is "that which magnetizes a desire for intimacy, sociality, affective solidarity, and happiness."

This may sound idealistic, yet the pervasive epidemic of loneliness today, along with soaring levels of clinical depression, suggest that the power of collectivity and the spirit of solidarity might be our best hope. Hope can come from the feeling that our actions matter, which explains why shared exuberance so often accompanies moments of intense collective endeavor. While helping to sustain individual confidence and preserve community life, greater openness to others also allows us to enjoy rather than fear diverse forms of inclusive hospitality, lessening our own inner terrors or sense of hollowness.

Rather than simply facilitating forms of predatory capitalism, which will always feed off ongoing calamities, the many present crises can encourage us to find better ways of seeking change together. Despite all impediments, watching the vitality of today's progressive movements—from radical eco-warriors to Black Lives Matter and disability rights activists, and the surge of union activism now occurring in the UK—I see some return to the longing for a better, more equitable world that defined earlier decades. The pleasure of acting in concert to assert our need for each other and our natural world can, and must, hold us together in the challenging years ahead. There may well be dark times, but there can also be singing, at least when we gather to work toward better futures.

CONTRIBUTORS

adrienne maree brown is an activist and author of *Holding Change: The Way of Emergent Strategy Facilitation and Mediation*, as well as the *New York Times* best-selling *Pleasure Activism: The Politics of Feeling Good*.

Breanne Fahs is Professor of Women and Gender Studies at Arizona State University and author of *Unshaved: Resistance & Revolution in Women's Body Hair Politics* and *Burn It Down!: Feminist Manifestos for the Revolution*. She is the Founder and Director of the Feminist Research on Gender and Sexuality Group at Arizona State University, and she also works as a clinical psychologist in private practice.

Jayati Ghosh is Professor of Economics at the University of Massachusetts Amherst and coauthor of the forthcoming book *Earth For All: A Survival Guide for Humanity*.

Jackson Lears is Professor of History at Rutgers University. His latest book, *Animal Spirits: The American Pursuit of Vitality*, is forthcoming from Farrar, Straus and Giroux.

Jonathan Levy is James Westfall Thompson Professor of U.S. History and Social Thought at the University of Chicago. His latest book is *Ages of American Capitalism: A History of the United States.*

Lida Maxwell is Associate Professor of Political Science and Women's, Gender, and Sexuality Studies at Boston University.

Micki McElya is Professor of History at the University of Connecticut and author of *Clinging to Mammy: The Faithful Slave in Twentieth-Century America* and *The Politics of Mourning: Death and Honor in Arlington National Cemetery*, which was a finalist for the 2017 Pulitzer Prize for General Non-Fiction. McElya is currently at work on her next book, *No More Miss America! How Protesting the 1968 Pageant Changed a Nation*, to be published by Avid Reader Press (Simon & Schuster).

Jennifer C. Nash is Jean Fox O'Barr Professor of Gender, Sexuality, and Feminist Studies at Duke University and author of *Birthing Black Mothers.*

Nanjala Nyabola is a writer and political analyst. Her most recent book is *Travelling While Black: Essays Inspired by a Life on the Move.*

Jack Parlett is author of *The Poetics of Cruising: Queer Visual Culture from Whitman to Grindr* and *Fire Island: A Century in the Life of an American Paradise*, which was named an Editor's Pick by the *New York Times*, as well as the poetry chapbook *Same Blue, Different You.*

His writing has appeared in the *New Yorker, Literary Hub, Poetry London*, and elsewhere.

Robert Pollin is Distinguished University Professor of Economics and Co-Director of the Political Economy Research Institute at the University of Massachusetts Amherst.

Will Rinehart is a Senior Research Fellow at the Center for Growth and Opportunity at Utah State University.

Ben Schacht is Audience Engagement Editor at *Boston Review*. He has written on literature and politics for *Jacobin, Synapsis: A Health Humanities Journal*, and *Majority Post*, among other publications.

Lynne Segal is Anniversary Professor Emerita of Psychosocial Studies at Birkbeck, University of London, author of *Radical Happiness: Moments of Collective Joy*, and coauthor of *The Care Manifesto: The Politics of Interdependence*.

Kate Soper is Emerita Professor of Philosophy at London Metropolitan University. She has been an editorial collective member of *Radical Philosophy* and of *New Left Review*, and a regular columnist for *Capitalism, Nature, Socialism*. She has translated works by Sebastiano Timpanaro, Noberto Bobbio, Michel Foucault, Cornelius Castoriadis, and Carlo Ginsburg. Her most recent books are *Post-Growth Living: for an Alternative Hedonism* and the coedited volumes *Citizenship and Consumption* and *The Politics and Pleasures of Consuming Differently*.